The Fund Raiser's Guide to Successful Campaigns

The Fund Raiser's Guide to Successful Campaigns

Ted D. Bayley

Vice President for Development
and Alumni Affairs
Georgia State University
Atlanta, Georgia

McGraw-Hill Book Company

New York   St. Louis   San Francisco   Auckland
Bogotá   Hamburg   London   Madrid   Mexico
Milan   Montreal   New Delhi   Panama
Paris   São Paulo   Singapore
Sydney   Tokyo   Toronto

Library of Congress Cataloging-in-Publication Data

Bayley, Ted D.
  The fund raiser's guide to successful campaigns.

  Includes index.
  1. Fund raising—United States—Handbooks,
manuals, etc. I. Title.
HV41.9.U5B39 1988   361.7′068′1   87-3188
ISBN 0-07-004118-0

1234567890   DOC/DOC   89210987

ISBN 0-07-004118-0

*The editors for this book were William A. Sabin and Virginia F. Blair,
the designer was Naomi Auerbach, and the production
supervisor was Dianne Walber. This book was set in Baskerville.
It was composed by the McGraw-Hill Book Company Professional
& Reference Division composition unit.*

Printed and bound by R. R. Donnelley & Sons Company.

Contents

Preface

"Who me? Raise money? Look, I'm willing to help the organization and I know we need money to operate, but I don't know how to raise money. Isn't that what we have staff people for?"

"As a board member I realize that I should help but others are much better at raising money than I am. Let me take on some other responsibility where I can really help."

"When I took this job as executive director, I did not understand that so much of my time would be spent trying to raise money. There must be some new ways we can get the help we need that won't make my job even harder."

If you have ever heard conversations like these or perhaps made similar statements yourself, then this book could be helpful to you. There are more than 300,000 nonprofit organizations and millions of volunteers that seek to secure money to operate every year. Sooner or later, they finally ask the people with the money—the citizens of our country.

Americans are generous! In 1985, individuals gave away more than $66 billion to churches, colleges, universities, the United Way, youth-serving agencies, community organizations, and national health causes. They did this out of their own pockets and pocketbooks. While some were undoubtedly influenced by the tax implications and by matching fund programs provided by many employers, most did it for one basic reason—someone they knew asked them for a contribution.

For well over 40 years, more than 80 percent of all the philanthropic dollars given away each year have come from individuals. Corporations, foundations, and bequests are important sources of support for non-profit organizations, and support from these sources is increasing; still, the most important source for nonprofit organizations continues to be individuals.

As a result of the values deeply rooted in the people who created our country, most Americans have developed a strong commitment to helping organizations and individuals when the need is clear and the cause is important. They give their time and their money to make things happen.

There are no secrets to raising money. Professional fund raisers have proved over and over that money can be raised for a broad array of causes when volunteers are organized into effective groups and seek the support of others.

Therefore, this book is mostly about people and how to organize and motivate them to ask others for financial support. It is designed to guide volunteers who are asked to help some organization raise money and for professionals who spend a good part of their time helping volunteers raise money. It should be especially helpful to employees of organizations who have reached a position of responsibility for helping secure the financial support needed each year.

By design, the book is not highly technical. For experienced fund raisers, both volunteer and professional, some of it may appear to be stating the obvious, and it does in many instances. For those with less experience, it should add some new understanding about how a group must organize to raise money. For all, I hope, it will give those who read it a feeling of optimism about the potential any organization has for securing adequate financial support when volunteers are organized to ask others for such support.

The book is divided into four parts. Part 1 deals with why people give money away, the characteristics of leadership necessary to raise money, and some general principles that can be applied to any organization, be it young or old, large or small.

Part 2 presents the basic organizational concepts for conducting an annual campaign to raise the dollars needed to operate for a year. If you are new to fund raising, you will find this section especially helpful. Even though you must design your own campaign around the structure of your own group, people will work together in productive teams to raise money when properly recruited, trained, and motivated.

Part 3 will give you some insights in how to solicit corporations, foundations, and individuals. Here you will see the general principles outlined in Chapter 3 interwoven into a process where your needs are presented to individuals who can make a contribution. The funds may come from a corporate officer, foundation director, or individual; at some point an individual or a very small group of people will make a decision to give you a contribution or not. If you have never asked anyone to make a contribution, you will find Chapter 8 especially helpful.

Part 4 covers special ways to raise money beyond the annual fund drive. For most organizations, some of these special campaigns may be useful annually in addition to your annual fund drive or, in the case of a capital funds campaign, may be used less frequently.

While any author would like to think that every chapter is important, the book is designed to help the reader get a quick review or overview of the concept and therefore does not need to be read in order. With the exception of Chapter 5, which has a strong link to Chapter 4, all other chapters stand alone and can be read as needed.

Included in a number of chapters are actual examples of materials used by successful organizations to raise money. I have also provided checklists or examples of how you might prepare your own material to support your campaign efforts. Where highly technical information will prove helpful, I have attempted to provide the names and addresses of professional organizations that can provide you with much more detail on the subject.

Ted D. Bayley

Acknowledgments

As I finish writing this manuscript, I realize, as have all other authors, no one writes any manuscript of this sort without the help and encouragement of many others. What I know, the skills that I have, and the experiences I have enjoyed are the result of many people helping me along the way. I became indebted early in my career in fund raising to three professional Scout executives: L. Pop Crow, Thomas R. Uffelman, and Ken Drupiewski. They gave me the training, experience, and inspiration I needed to learn how to recruit and motivate people.

As I began to think about writing a book on the subject, Kenneth Black, Jr., and R. Cary Bynum were very helpful in development of the structure of the book and its presentation.

Special thanks go to Richard D. Martinides, Ralph A. Beck, Fred A. Tillman, Francis W. Rushing, Janis K. Robson, John W. Henderson, Glenn W. Summerlin, Anne Deeley, Richard B. Dillard, Mary Kay Murphy, and Laurelynn Moore for their help in technical review and helpful comments on the material.

In the final analysis, I could not have done it without the support and encouragement of my wife, Ellen.

Most of all, I am indebted to the thousands of volunteers who have worked in the campaigns with which I have been associated over the years. Their enthusiasm, commitment, and willingness to do most any job has been an inspiration. On more than one occasion, when the goal seemed unattainable or the task too large, some volunteer stepped forward and said "Let me help." These people are the real "teachers."

PART 1

Basic Concepts of Fund Raising

French author Alexis de Tocqueville noted over 100 years ago in his now classic book, *Democracy in America*, that Americans were a people that formed associations. They joined together to accomplish objectives that were important to them. They pooled their personal resources, and they raised money to help address a specific issue or solve a specific problem.

While giving to charity does exist in other societies, nowhere else in the world does it exist at the level that it does in America.

Chapters 1, 2, and 3 give you some idea of why people give money away, how they organize as volunteers to secure these gifts, and the general principles that motivate people to give.

1
Understanding the Donor Market

Who Gives Money?

Individuals continue to give more than 80 percent of all funds donated to charitable organizations, institutions, and agencies. While major grants from foundations, corporations, or bequests often make the news, without individuals annually making personal contributions, the churches, schools, hospitals, arts, and social welfare organizations throughout the United States could not operate. The 1985 Annual Report of the American Association of Fund-Raising Counsel, Inc., stated that individuals accounted for $66.06 billion in contributions during 1985. This 8.9 percent increase over the previous year represented real growth for most organizations, as the rate of inflation was only 3.7 percent. (See Tables 1.1 and 1.2.)

For many decades, individual donors have provided the major amount of contributed dollars. The American Association of Fund-Raising Counsel, Inc., notes that even with this long record of generosity, two people out of five feel that they do not give enough.[1]

Why People Give Money

It is clear that Americans are generous people. Understanding why is difficult, and the little research there is into what motivates individuals to donate part of their earned income is very limited in scope. Dr. Sidney J. Levy has suggested, in an article entitled "Humanized Appeals in

Table 1.1. 1985 Philanthropy

Contributions (billions)		Contributions as % of total
Individuals	$66.06	82.7
Bequests	5.18	6.5
Foundations	4.30	5.4
Corporations	4.30	5.4
Distributions (billions)		Distributions as % of total
Religion	$37.73	47.2
Health and hospitals	11.25	14.1
Education	11.05	13.8
Social welfare	8.56	10.7
Arts and humanities	5.09	6.4
Civic and public	2.24	2.8
Other	3.92	4.9

SOURCE: American Association of Fund-Raising Counsel, Inc., *Giving USA: Estimates of Philanthropic Giving in 1985 and the Trends They Show.*

Fund Raising" published in the July 1960 *Public Relations Journal,* that the two primary motivating factors are a sense of duty and personal self-interest. He discovered that people were reared with a sense of responsibility toward helping others. From childhood, people are taught to share their toys and their candy. As they grow older, these behavior patterns become a sense of duty toward those "less fortunate." Levy also

Table 1.2. Giving by Individuals

Year	Amount (billions)	Personal income (billions)	% of income
1970	$16.19	$ 831.8	1.95
1971	17.64	894.0	1.97
1972	19.37	981.6	1.97
1973	20.53	1,101.7	1.86
1974	21.60	1,210.1	1.79
1975	23.53	1,313.4	1.79
1976	26.32	1,451.4	1.81
1977	29.55	1,607.5	1.84
1978	32.10	1,812.4	1.77
1979	36.59	2,034.0	1.80
1980	40.71	2,258.5	1.80
1981	46.42	2,520.9	1.84
1982	48.52	2,670.8	1.82
1983	53.54	2,836.4	1.89
1984	60.66	3,111.9	1.95
1985	66.06	3,294.2	2.01

SOURCE: American Association of Fund-Raising Counsel, Inc., *Giving USA: Estimates of Philanthropic Giving in 1985 and the Trends They Show.*

discovered that a strong element of self-interest motivated many givers. Contributors developed a "personal sense of well-being," and sharing with others made them "feel good." They were also strongly influenced by religious teachings and often felt they were "buying a place in Heaven" or giving in repentance for sins.[2]

One is always reluctant to suggest that *all* giving is motivated by self-interest—and in the process exclude altruism as a motivating factor for some people. One could argue that altruism is demonstrated daily as caring people open their pocketbooks to help those in distress. Giving a few coins to the blind person on the street corner provides the giver no public recognition, no membership in an organization, and no enhanced social position, but since it does make the person "feel good" or remove some level of guilt, one could argue that even this gift is motivated by self-interest.

Hierarchy of Loyalty

Levy's research also suggested a hierarchy of loyalty that is helpful to those who seek to raise contributed dollars. The individual's church has the highest loyalty. Slightly more than 47 percent of all contributed dollars go to religious organizations. This has been a consistent pattern for over 30 years. Second only to religious organizations are the fraternal groups, schools, and social groups to which the individual belongs. In both categories, the individual has a sense of "ownership," a feeling that he or she "belongs to the group."

Emotionally related groups, such as health care agencies, national organizations seeking to cure or prevent disease, and social agencies "helping the less fortunate," form the third group in the hierarchy. The obligatory group, the fourth level in the hierarchy of loyalty, includes the United Way and the Red Cross. Apparently, many individuals see these two organizations as fund raisers who provide income to other organizations who help people. Since the two national organizations often solicit in the workplace, using payroll deduction, contributors, like it or not, feel obligated to contribute so as not to lose favor with employers.

The lower two elements of the hierarchy suggest individuals may be concerned with "prevention," and their contributions demonstrate their concern for solving problems.

If one accepts Levy's hierarchy of loyalty, it is reasonable to conclude that any organization seeking contributed dollars from individuals can improve the likelihood of successful response by positioning itself, in the minds of the contributor, as far up the hierarchy as possible. Therefore, organizations that provide a sense of membership or ownership will improve their chances for contributions, even though the services they provide might suggest a lower position on the hierarchy.

Experience of Fund Raisers

Another way to understand why people give money is to study the past 100 years' experience of professional fund raisers and organizations. An experienced fund raiser will state that "people give to people." The implication of that experience is very important. People find it extremely difficult to turn down a request for a contribution made by a peer or a personal friend. If this relationship exists between the solicitor and the potential contributor, the cause or organization tends to become secondary. Simply put, people give when they are asked for a gift. Very few people contribute to an organization without being asked to or reminded of the organization's financial needs.

Recent Research Gives New Insights

A national survey conducted in 1985 and funded by the Rockefeller Brothers Fund provides confirmation of earlier research and experience of professional fund raisers. It also provides some new insights that are important.

The research confirmed that personal solicitation by a friend is still the best way to raise money, especially with large givers. The report noted, "When large donors were asked what solicitation approach they were most likely to respond to, over 75 percent responded that they were likely to give when a person they knew well asked them to."[3]

Those organizations seeking annual contributions to operate their programs must recognize the utmost importance of the implications of this principle. It is vital that an organization needing annual support develop a sufficient base of contributors to make annual contributions to its operations. Annual financial support by individuals strongly indicates broad-based support and often becomes the critical factor in securing United Way, foundation, and corporate grants.

The study also found that volunteer participation in the organization leads to increased giving. Pledging and payroll deduction are important factors in securing larger gifts as well. Discretionary income also influences contributions. People who perceive that they have a moderate amount of discretionary income give more than those who feel that they only have enough to cover basic needs. Also, people who worry about their economic future give less than those who feel secure about their economic future.[4]

A broad base of annual contributions clearly indicates the viability of the organization's work. It also provides a criterion for evaluating the effectiveness and efficiency of the organization in providing its service and communicating with its supporters. If the donors do not see the organization as beneficial or effective in meeting a need that they can identify with, securing annual contributions will be more difficult and reduced contributions will normally result.

Establishing Donor Potential

Establishing the donor potential must be the first order of business for an organization seeking contributed dollars for its annual operation. Some might argue that the entire adult population of the community, state, region, or nation is its potential donor market, but this is rarely a realistic approach.

Acknowledge Limits

It is impossible to contact everyone given the limited resources available in the organization. From time to time one will see an all but unknown organization secure sufficient funding to make a direct mail solicitation to hundreds of thousands of people. Since response rates in direct mail solicitation to a list that size rarely exceed 1 to 3 percent, it is naive to believe that most organizations can find successful financial support by seeking to contact every individual in a given area by mail. This is not to imply that direct mail solicitation is inappropriate. Many organizations use direct mail solicitation successfully, but it is rarely the sole source of support for the organization. Additional material on direct mail solicitation appears in Chapter 10.

Likewise, while telethons may appear to reach everyone, they don't. And even with significant donated time and talent, they are expensive and rarely appropriate for most organizations seeking annual support. Like direct mail, telethons are usually one of several sources of income for those organizations that conduct them.

Approach Service Recipients

If an organization has a reason to exist, it has a starting base for potential contributors. Assuming the organization provides a service to some clientele, the recipients of the service are the obvious first source of potential contributors. For example, many colleges and universities that seek contributions from their alumni now solicit parents of students currently enrolled for contributions to their annual campaign as well. Similarly, youth-service agencies such as the Boy Scouts, Girl Scouts, and the YMCAs and YWCAs often seek contributions from the parents of youngsters in their programs. Many hospitals seek contributions from former patients or families of patients.

Even organizations serving clients in reduced or desperate financial conditions may find it possible to develop potential funding from friends, employers, or community groups that identify with the clients. It is not unusual for those of limited means to support the organizations that helped them in the past with small contributions. The American Association of Fund-Raising Counsel noted in its 1985 Annual Report that "61 million low- and moderate-income Americans who do not itemize deductions on their tax returns provided $22 billion in charitable gifts in 1984. That amount represented 35 percent of all money donated by individuals and 30 percent of all donations to charitable organizations by individuals, foundations, and corporations according to this estimate."[5]

Use the Board of Directors

For most organizations the best starting point in developing a donor base is its board of directors, each of whom wants the organization to operate successfully. Each board member has personal friends who are potential contributors if the board member seeks their contributions. Further, most board members have business relationships that lead to potential prospects. Probably the best "names" that will come from a board member are those who have solicited the board member for a contribution for an organization they represent.

When you first involve your board in a fund-raising effort, questions will be raised about the proper role of the board. Some people who have agreed to serve on your board are very uncomfortable when asked to help raise the necessary funds to operate each year. Some will suggest that they give their time and do not feel that they should be asked to make gifts to the organization. Some will be concerned that there may be members that cannot afford to give money to your campaign. When these concerns are raised, most often, they are really concerns about the individuals' fear of asking others to make a gift. Be sensitive to this, but help the board understand their role in fund raising. Not every member of the board may be asked for the same gift. Each member should be

evaluated just as you evaluate other prospects. However, having every
member contribute is extremely important. Your board *must* set the
example. I would expect all staff to also make their pledges before the
campaign starts. You do not have to have every board member making
a major gift annually, but asking others to give is easier when you can
report 100 percent commitment from the board and the staff. Besides,
contributing board members take a more active role in your organization than do non-contributors. Long-term success of nonprofit organizations requires a committed board.

Securing Your Initial List

To develop your starting list, the board members must understand the
importance of a contributor base and must make a commitment to help
the annual campaign succeed. Most boards have some members that are
more productive in adding names to a prospect list, but all can add some
if they are motivated to do so.

Figure 1.1 is a sample that you can reproduce to start developing your
initial list. It includes the name of the person completing it, since this
person may be the best solicitor when the campaign begins. The
information needed includes the correct name (spelled correctly, an
often overlooked detail in fund raising), complete address, and zip code.
A telephone number will also be very helpful later in the campaign.

On the initial gathering of this information, little else is needed.
Additional information will be added to the prospect's file as the
prospect card and campaign records are developed prior to the start of
the campaign.

Ask the Advice of Others

Beyond the board of directors are often other groups within the
organization, including staff, volunteer leaders, community advisory
groups, and retired employees. Many of these individuals will be glad to
provide names of potential prospects if asked.

Public Sources

Finally, the organization can develop lists of potential prospects from
public sources, including city directories, chamber of commerce membership lists, civic club rosters, and donor lists published by other
nonprofit organizations in the community. Lists like these indicate the

Potential Prospect Form				
Submitted by			Date	
Name	Address	City	ZIP	Phone

Figure 1.1. Potential prospect form

names of involved people in the community. They are the most likely prospects for donations. As they become supporters of your organization, they may provide sources of additional names.

When you develop prospect lists from sources such as these, be careful to do good research and get accurate information from public sources. Set up a system to avoid duplication of names. No one likes to be asked by two or three people for a contribution to the same campaign, and likewise, no solicitor likes to hear "I just gave to your organization last week." Also remember that you will need to evaluate the names as to giving potential so that the right solicitor is assigned to the card. More details related to prospect selection and evaluation appear in Chapter 4.

One final thought: Although most Americans properly cultivated and solicited are potential contributors to worthy causes, many of your best prospects are likely to already be contributors to the other community organizations. In many cases your financial supporters will also be supporters of alumni associations, the arts, medical causes, the United Way, and other civic causes.

Notes

1. Richard Piperno and Fred Schnaue, *Giving USA: Estimates of Philanthropic Giving in 1985 and the Trends They Show*, American Association of Fund-Raising Counsel, Inc., New York, 1986, p. 11, (published annually).

2. Sidney J. Levy, "Humanized Appeals in Fund Raising," *Public Relations Journal*, vol. XVI, July 1960, no. 7, p. 17.

3. Virginia Ann Hodgkinson and Murray S. Weitzman, *The Charitable Behavior of Americans: Findings from a National Survey*, Independent Sector, Washington, D.C., 1985, p. 53.

4. Ibid., p. 52.

5. *Giving USA*, p. 16.

2
Organizing to Raise Money

Who Raises Money?

In a word, volunteers! While some large nonprofit organizations have a great deal of staff support and often the personal involvement of key senior staff members, such as the executive director or development director, in making solicitation calls, the role of the volunteer is fundamental.

The volunteer, who may be an alumnus, board member, patron, benefactor, officer, or friend, participates in the solicitation of a friend or peer because of a personal belief in and commitment to the programs and objectives of the organization. This personal participation plays a key role in securing gifts to the organization. A volunteer asking for a contribution adds credibility to the request that is otherwise missing. Even though the story can be told and the gift requested by staff members, the impact of the volunteer in many cases ensures a gift. The role of professional staff is to facilitate the organization and effective conducting of the campaign. Their help—in most cases behind the scenes—involves planning, training, and motivating volunteer leaders.

Good campaign leadership usually occurs in organizations with a lot of community interest and high visibility. The names of these leaders appear in the local news media frequently. Typically, these leaders will be involved in education, politics, commerce, women's groups, religion, labor, and community agencies. When you mention these leaders in a small group, several people recognize their names and usually someone knows one or more of them. To be successful over time, you must stay abreast of community leadership on a regular basis by reading newspapers and related community publications.

What Makes a Good Money Raiser?

Successful fund-raising volunteers come in all shapes, sizes, sexes, races, religions, and economic circumstances. Initially most volunteers become involved in the work of the organization and want to see it prosper, expand, and serve its clientele. Few, at the beginning, have had experience in the actual solicitation process for fund raising.

When you seek successful fund-raising volunteers, be aware that they share several common characteristics.

Proven Leadership

The first characteristic, leadership experience, can be as a volunteer in a community group or similar activity, in employment or profession, or in political, religious, or educational groups. Successful fund-raising campaigns must have people with proven leadership and organizational skills if the campaign is to be successful.

Involvement

The second, involvement, can be illustrated by an old fund-raising axiom: "If you have an important job to do, ask a busy person." The kind of persons with solid leadership you are seeking are almost always involved in community activities. They teach Sunday school, sing in choirs, chair PTA committees, work with band booster associations, lead in United Way campaigns, serve as officers in service organizations, manage successful companies or organizations, and participate in good causes. The bigger the job in the fund-raising campaign, the busier the person asked to assume the job is likely to be.

Commitment

The third characteristic, commitment, means good volunteer fund raisers believe in what they are doing. They believe that the organization provides worthwhile services to people and the community. They believe in their important role and feel a strong sense of identity with the organization. They subscribe to the axiom "put your money where your mouth is," and many make significant contributions in addition to general support of the organization.

Community Recognition

The fourth characteristic, community recognition, means that peers and other community leaders know them as leaders, involved and committed to the good of the community and its people. They can reach other community leaders on the phone. They see other community leaders at meetings, concerts, and similar gatherings they attend. They often serve on boards and other leadership bodies within the community. People seek their advice whenever a problem must be addressed.

Organizing the Campaign Team

Any successful fund-raising campaign depends on identifying, recruiting, and organizing campaign leadership. Poor results here reduce success. Good results—getting the right top volunteer—convert an annual chore into an exciting experience.

Finding the General Campaign Chairperson

Oversight of securing the financial support necessary for the organization may be the responsibility of a board officer, typically a vice president. If your organization's bylaws do assign this responsibility, you must make sure that the officer provides the leadership capabilities discussed. If not, you must find alternative ways to use that officer as an advisor and recruit a top campaign leader who has the necessary characteristics. Because the campaign leadership has such importance, you cannot automatically accept leadership that comes from officership unless the officer can do the job—completely and effectively.

Appointing an Obvious Choice. Your basic objective in starting a campaign to raise money must be to secure the personal commitment of the best person available to lead the campaign. If your choice is not a board member and you can add your candidate to the board immediately, do so. If not, have the board or its president appoint the person to this important position.

Starting from Scratch.   If you have no board member or other readily apparent choice, develop a small prospect list and evaluate it with board members—preferably in a small group meeting where discussion suggests additional candidates who could do the job or play a part in some phase of the campaign.

If you are starting from scratch, follow this proven sequence:

1. *Make a list.*   List the names of those who led recent successful campaigns for other organizations. Who led the United Negro College Fund campaign, the Heart Fund Drive, the Campaign for Support of the Arts, or the United Way campaign last year? Who led previous highly successful campaigns in your organization? These leaders may be available. Recognized community leaders often respond to this type of opportunity.

2. *Rate the prospects.*   Take your list, review the characteristics you need with your key volunteers, and rate your prospects. Add the rating to the list. Write the names on a flip chart or chalkboard so everyone can see them. Discussion leads to more names. Rank and rate those names also. Develop a priority list of four to six names, with the most qualified at the top and others in descending order of qualifications.

3. *Convince your choice.*   Determine who in your organization can get a positive response from each prospect. A board member, friend of the organization, or past campaign chairperson all make good choices.

   a. *Schedule a meeting.*   Make an appointment and call on your top prospect. Take your board's senior officer, the organization's executive director, and the person you believe can get a positive response.

   b. *Present your case.*   Briefly outline the organization's work and ask the prospect to accept the job, emphasizing your board's view that his or her leadership can ensure continued success. Discuss your financial needs and briefly review the campaign organization and timetable.

   c. *Take a job description.*   A brief job description (Figure 2.1) outlining major responsibilities and key campaign dates helps gain acceptance. Don't pull punches! You *do not* want someone to "make a few phone calls." You need active, enthusiastic campaign leadership from beginning to end. Telling the whole story up front evokes a much more supportive response.

   d. *Describe the support network.*   Describe what support the board and staff provide during the campaign. Estimate the time required as accurately as possible. Reinforce the importance of the prospect's leadership and its impact on the organization's work.

e. *Review the selection process.* Convince the prospect by briefly reviewing the selection process the board used to identify the right person. This communicates both the importance of the job and the respect your board has for the person.

f. *Keep it short.* What sounds like a long presentation should not be. Plan *who* covers *what.* Practice the presentation. State your case briefly, clearly, and accurately. Cover essentials with minimal detail. Limit your request to 3 to 5 minutes. A prospect who wants to know more before deciding will ask questions. Be prepared to provide more detail in this dialogue.

4. *Follow-up on acceptance or rejection.* If your prospect accepts, schedule a follow-up meeting. Set the date before you leave if possible. This reinforces the commitment. Assure the new chairperson of your group's readiness to provide full support. If you get a no, thank the prospect for seeing you and set an appointment with your next prospect. Rarely will you go through five names without a yes—provided you have followed the process carefully.

a. *Make a current no a future yes.* Even if you get a no, you may get a future commitment or help in another campaign phase. Remember this and use the information appropriately.

b. *Accept the help offered.* Keep in mind that everyone on your list makes an excellent prospect for campaign gifts. Often the person who says no suggests a contribution in lieu of active leadership. Take advantage of the opportunity by having a pledge card with you, and some consensus about the amount to request and who from your group will ask for the gift.

Recruiting the Campaign Steering Committee

You may need several levels of leadership, depending on the scope and size of the campaign. Almost certainly your chairperson will want and need a vice chairperson. A campaign steering committee, explained in detail in Chapter 4, rounds out the group that provides the overall leadership of the campaign. These important leaders make the job of the general chairperson "doable." The chairperson's *first* responsibility must be helping identify and personally recruiting this team. If the chairperson personally recruits the team, you will have much less chance of poor follow-up by members of the team during the campaign. If you have a problem with a person on the team, have the chairperson call, and in most cases procrastination disappears. If you do the recruiting for the chairperson, nonperformance becomes *your problem.* Have suggestions ready for each assignment on the steering committee, but remember that the chairperson may already have people in mind to include. Be prepared to include them.

Job Descriptions Are the Key

Provide written job descriptions for each position to help the chairperson understand the type of people to recruit. Job descriptions also help exclude unqualified candidates if the chairperson suggests any such names for the steering committee.

With the campaign steering committee in place, additional layers of leadership will be needed. Again, depending on the size and scope of the campaign, you may need dozens or even hundreds of volunteers. Structure the campaign organization so that no one is personally recruiting more than five or six helpers. Expecting much beyond this makes the recruiting job a real burden on the volunteer and leads to discouraging results.

Written job descriptions for all volunteer jobs in the campaign organization are most helpful. These must be custom-developed for your organization and will remain essentially the same from year to year. They usually list four or five major responsibilities, such as recruit five campaign solicitors, personally encourage your team to participate in the campaign orientation and kickoff meeting on March 1, make weekly contacts with your team, attend the report meetings. Examples of such job descriptions are found in Figures 2.1 through 2.5.

Make sure that the job descriptions clearly spell out the responsibilities being accepted, the specific deadlines called for, and to whom the person is responsible. Include specific dates for key campaign events in the job description if possible.

XYZ ORGANIZATION

ANNUAL FUND-RAISING CAMPAIGN 19XX

JOB DESCRIPTION: General Campaign Chairperson

YOUR JOB:

1. You are responsible to the governing board of the XYZ Organization, John H. Smith, president.
2. Follow the campaign plan and calendar of action.
3. Recruit chairs by November 12, 19XX for:
   Audit   Facilities
   Training   Communications
   Prospects and rating   Solicitation
4. Submit their names, addresses, and phone numbers to the campaign office.
5. Conduct a training session for the steering committee by December 1, 19XX.
6. Become knowledgeable about the financial needs of the XYZ Organization so as to inspire a positive atmosphere for success.
7. Make your own pledge before recruiting others.
8. Be in frequent and regular contact with your committee chairs to ensure that the campaign stays on schedule.
9. Chair regular meetings of the steering committee and the campaign report meetings according to the schedule.
10. Chair the victory meeting with your steering committee.

Figure 2.1. Job Description—General Chair

XYZ ORGANIZATION

ANNUAL FUND-RAISING CAMPAIGN 19XX

JOB DESCRIPTION: Solicitation Chairperson

YOUR JOB:

1. You are responsible to: Sam I. Wilson, general campaign chairperson for the campaign.
2. Follow the campaign plan and calendar of action.
3. Recruit five division chairpersons to head five solicitation divisions by January 5, 19XX.
4. Submit their names, addresses, and phone numbers to the campaign office.
5. Become knowledgeable about the budget and needs of the XYZ Organization so as to inspire a positive attitude for success.
6. Make your own pledge to the campaign before recruiting others.
7. Stay in frequent contact with your division chairpersons and encourage them to meet the deadlines established for the campaign.
8. Attend the training meeting with your division chairpersons scheduled for January 18, 19XX.
9. Attend the kickoff meeting with your division chairpersons scheduled for March 1, 19XX.
10. Attend all report meetings for your division.
11. Attend the victory meeting with your division chairpersons.

Figure 2.2.   Job Description—Solicitation Chair

XYZ ORGANIZATION

ANNUAL FUND-RAISING CAMPAIGN 19XX

JOB DESCRIPTION: <u>Division Chairperson</u>

YOUR JOB:

1. You are responsible to Ruth C. Green, solicitation chairperson for the campaign.
2. Follow the campaign plan and calendar of action.
3. Recruit five captains to head five solicitation teams by <u>February 1, 19XX</u>.
4. Submit their names, addresses, and phone numbers to the campaign office.
5. Become knowledgeable about the budget and needs of the XYZ Organization so as to inspire a positive attitude for success.
6. Make your own pledge before recruiting others.
7. Stay in frequent contact with your captains and encourage them to meet the deadlines established for the campaign.
8. Attend the training meeting with your captains scheduled for <u>February 8, 19XX</u>.
9. Attend the kickoff meeting with your captains scheduled for <u>March 1, 19XX</u>.
10. Attend all report meetings with your captains.
11. Attend the victory meeting with your captains.

Figure 2.3.   Job Description—Division Chair

XYZ ORGANIZATION

ANNUAL FUND-RAISING CAMPAIGN 19XX

JOB DESCRIPTION: <u>Captain</u>

YOUR JOB:

1. You are responsible to George C. Brown, division chairperson.
2. Follow the campaign plan and calendar of action.
3. Recruit five solicitors by <u>February 15, 19XX</u>.
4. Submit their names, addresses, and phone numbers to the campaign office.
5. Attend the orientation and kickoff meeting with your solicitors scheduled for <u>March 1, 19XX</u>.
6. Become knowledgeable about the budget and needs of the XYZ Organization so as to inspire a positive attitude for success.
7. Stay in frequent contact with your solicitors and encourage them to make their calls before the scheduled report meetings.
8. Make your own pledge before recruiting others.
9. Attend the victory meeting with your solicitors.

Figure 2.4.   Job Description—Captain

XYZ ORGANIZATION

ANNUAL FUND-RAISING CAMPAIGN 19XX

JOB DESCRIPTION: Solicitor

YOUR JOB:

1. You are responsible to Ellen K. Johnson, captain.
2. Follow the campaign plan and calendar of action.
3. Attend the orientation and kickoff meeting scheduled for March 1, 19XX.
4. Select five prospect cards and make personal calls on them by April 1, 19XX.
5. Submit your completed pledge cards to your captain at the report meetings.
6. Become knowledgeable about the budget and needs of the XYZ Organization so as to inspire a positive attitude for success.
7. Make your own pledge before calling on your prospects.
8. Attend the victory meeting.

Figure 2.5.   Job Description—Solicitor

Additional Organizational Elements

Some groups find geographic area the most effective organizational principle; others use "gift size" or a combination of the two. Much more about organizational techniques appears in Chapter 4. For now, keep in mind that the characteristics presented earlier apply to all leadership roles regardless of the level. Always go for the best available person.

3

Ten Principles for Successful Fund Raising

No list of principles as they relate to human behavior can be absolute. Similarly, no list of principles that relate to organization and individual motivation can be comprehensive. Experienced fund raisers or development officers conclude that the following 10 principles describe human behavior and affect the outcome of fund-raising activities.

While these principles could be stated somewhat differently, you must understand and acknowledge these underlying principles if you want to provide leadership for successful fund-raising campaigns.

1. Personal Solicitation of Each Prospect

While there are dozens of ways to "solicit" prospects for donations, nothing beats the personal request for a contribution. Further, the chances of securing a contribution are dramatically increased when the solicitor is a friend or a business or social peer of the person solicited. "People give to people" is a phrase used by many fund raisers and is another way of stating this principle. While a positive image of the organization in the mind of the prospect is helpful, the personal request of a friend for support of a cause, program, or organization will have more impact on the prospect than knowledge of the organization.

Recent research shows that more than 75 percent of all Americans who contribute $500 or more a year will likely make a donation when asked by a friend.[1]

Ideally, every prospect would be solicited by a personal friend. Obviously, in most campaigns this is not possible. In these situations it is important to come as close as possible to meeting the full intent of this principle as solicitors make their contacts. While the prospect being called on may not be a "personal friend" of the solicitor, he or she may be acquainted with the individual through professional relationships in the business community or social relationships through common activities such as church involvement, school activities, or alumni activities.

Once you are committed to face-to-face solicitation, it also becomes extremely important to match the giving capacity of the solicitor to the anticipated giving capacity of the prospect. The person being solicited for a specific amount of money should be called on by a solicitor who has already made a similar financial commitment to the campaign.

2. Good Solicitors Are Trained and Knowledgeable

Many volunteer organizations will have a cadre of volunteers deeply committed to the activities, programs, and objectives of the organization. However, the majority of these committed volunteers have no experience in asking others to contribute to the support of the organization. Most committed volunteers will find it easy to talk about the programs and the successes of the organization, but they will not know how to ask for a contribution. Therefore, individuals who agree to serve as campaign solicitors must have training in how to request a gift. Never assume that previous campaign workers know how to ask for a gift. Quite often the contrary is true. While they may have called on some prospects in a previous campaign, the level of support they obtained may not have been as good as it could have been with a better presentation.

3. All Solicitors Make Their Contributions First

It is both unfair to the solicitor and unproductive to the organization to expect individuals to ask others to give contributions to the organization if the solicitor has not already made a personal financial commitment. A person's contribution is evidence of commitment to the objectives of the organization. We would be shocked to enter a Ford dealership and find that the sales manager drives a Chevrolet. Our assumption would be that the sales manager of the Ford dealership would be committed to that company's product. So why should a volunteer solicitor be less committed?

Not only should the solicitor make his or her personal commitment, it should be made during the campaign-recruiting or training phase. Securing this commitment also plays another important role. Since personal peer solicitation is fundamental to a good campaign success, the volunteer's commitment gives a clear indication as to the dollar level of prospect cards that should be assigned to this particular solicitor.

4. Quality Leadership Ensures Success

This principle is fundamental for the successful management of any enterprise and is of critical importance for nonprofit organizations seeking to secure donations from the public. Strong campaign leadership will be required to recruit, motivate, and lead a large group of volunteers in accomplishing the objectives of the campaign. This means the leadership must be willing to devote sufficient time and energy to ensure the accomplishment of its total campaign objectives. Because it is a volunteer organization, campaign leadership must be willing to make changes of assignment among volunteer leaders as needed, while continuing to encourage and motivate the entire organizational structure. Top campaign leadership is always found in key leadership roles within community organizations and business enterprise.

A successful leader is fully committed to the organization, is recognized as a leader in the community, and has been a part of successful campaigns for your organization or similar community organizations in the past.

5. Volunteer-Established Goals for Dollars and Contributors

If campaign leadership is to motivate volunteers to reach objectives in dollars raised and prospects contacted, these volunteers must have a voice in the development of these objectives. Volunteer organizations can effectively use the "management by objectives" (MBO) principles that are commonly utilized in the business community. If a volunteer participates in the development of objectives, he or she will be much more committed to reaching those objectives. I do not recall ever working with a key volunteer in a campaign who took the job to fail! Volunteers want and expect to reach the goal.

One must be skillful in leading volunteer groups to establish the necessary objectives. Keep in mind that volunteers, without proper leadership, will tend to establish goals that are too low to reach the total objectives of the campaign—or so high they are unreachable. Objectives established at either extreme are unacceptable for successful campaigning. Volunteer solicitors need to feel the success of reaching campaign objectives; they will quickly lose interest in a campaign when it appears to them that the objectives are unrealistic or impossible to attain. Likewise, they will "go the extra mile" when the objective is in sight, identifying additional prospects or making that one last visit.

Contributor goals may be as important as dollar goals to your organization. A large base of financial support is of critical importance to the ongoing operation of most nonprofit organizations. While securing the dollar objective with one large gift might seem like a blessing, it does not provide stable financial support for the organization. Each contributor to this year's campaign becomes an excellent prospect for next year's campaign. Emphasize with volunteers that asking for the gift is also important because of the educational value for the prospective donor.

The annual campaign is partly "friend making." For a number of years, the American Cancer Society, one of the pioneers of the door-to-door campaign technique, doggedly stuck to direct neighbor-to-neighbor solicitation because the educational value was as important to their organization's objectives as was the securing of gifts. While the social environment has changed to the point where it has become difficult, if not impossible, for direct door-to-door solicitation in many communities, the underlying principle of educating individuals about the work of the organization is still a valid one. Victory in a good campaign is reached when dollar and contributor goals are met and exceeded!

6. Keep Campaigns Fun, Quick, and On Schedule

By nature, most of us are procrastinators. When an organization seeks to use volunteers in soliciting donations, procrastination becomes an even bigger problem. It's quite natural to put off those things we don't like to do or don't know how to do. For many volunteers, the thought of asking someone else for a contribution leads to procrastination. The fundamental technique that moves one from procrastinator to solicitor is the campaign schedule. Target dates understood by all solicitors will force action. The original idea of the annual campaign pioneered by the YMCA in the 1890s was developed because volunteer board members got tired of begging for money all year long and were concerned about delivering program not raising money. By creating the campaign idea of conducting a fund-raising effort over a relatively short period of time, the organization generated excitement among volunteers and dramatically increased community response. Volunteers working together to raise money love to "win." Reaching the goal, on schedule, gives everyone a feeling of success.

In addition to a short time frame, it's also important that volunteers have fun while raising money. Friendly competition among soliciting teams, music, door prizes, gag gifts, recognition newsletters, all add an element of fun and fellowship. Since we tend to do those things we like to do, the element of fun also ensures that the level of procrastination is reduced.

7. Ask Prospects for a Specific Gift

One of the most misunderstood principles in raising money is the necessity of asking for a specific gift. "Will you consider joining me in giving $500 to the YMCA?" illustrates exactly how specific the request should be. Obviously, one would not ask every prospect for $500, thus the need to evaluate the giving potential of all prospects. The request for the specific amount places the prospect in a decision role. He or she knows that a gift is requested, and the amount becomes a frame of reference. If the solicitor is a friend or peer, the prospect probably knows of the involvement of the solicitor in the organization's work and will give the request serious consideration. It also places the prospect in a position of having to respond. A typical response is to say yes or to ask a question. Many volunteers are willing to ask for "your help with this campaign" or "a gift," but they get nervous at requesting a specific amount. Without a specific amount, the prospect must still deal with uncertainty. Remember, your solicitors are helped over this reluctance because they will have already contributed at the same level. A specific amount also carries an unspoken message that includes the following elements: (1) this is an important program worthy of your support, (2) you are an important person, and (3) I want you to join me in this effort.

Techniques for evaluating prospects are explained in Chapter 4. For the moment, one should understand that in keeping with principles 1 and 3, a solicitor who has made a $100 commitment to the organization should be calling on prospects who, if properly motivated, are capable of giving a like amount of money. It is a waste of valuable talent to ask an individual who has already made a personal commitment of $100 to call on individuals who are likely to be $5 contributors. Likewise, it would be unproductive to ask an individual solicitor who has made a $100 commitment to influence $500 potential prospects to make their donations. Always match the solicitor with the prospect and request an amount.

8. Campaigns Require Personal Follow-up

There is no alternative to personal follow-up by campaign leadership. Newsletters, telephone calls from staff, pep rallies, and the like are helpful but do not accomplish the total motivation necessary. More simply put, the person who recruited the solicitor is personally responsible for the successful performance of that solicitor.

Campaign leadership must expect timely performance of the task assigned. In a multilevel campaign involving hundreds of volunteers this means that the campaign chairperson is responsible for recruiting and motivating the people he or she recruits for certain functions within the campaign, and they in a similar manner are responsible for recruiting and motivating the volunteers that work on their teams in the campaign's operation. Volunteers and organizations have the right to expect personal performance from individuals if they agree to help. There is no better person to ensure that performance than the volunteer who recruited the campaign worker.

9. Donors Must Feel a Sense of Identity

Nonprofit organizations live or die on consistent financial support. Donors will continue their support over time when they feel a sense of identity with your organization. Research has shown clearly that people give more to those organizations that they personally identify with and less to those that they feel are simply "good for the community." Therefore, symbols of personal involvement greatly enhance the success of the annual fund-raising campaign. These symbols can include recognition plaques, membership cards, and a personal thank-you letter; each of these helps the person feel a part of the organization. In addition,

such techniques as seeking contributor advice on potential new programs and inviting contributors to board meetings or other activities of
the organization will help. In some organizations, contributors become
voting members for purposes of an annual meeting to elect board
members and officers and to make changes to the organization's bylaws.
The contributors are treated somewhat like stockholders in a corporation. Your annual meeting can also be one of receiving activity reports,
recognition reports, recognition of volunteer service, and induction of
new board members. Find some way to help your contributors feel a
sense of partnership.

While some volunteers will profess quite humbly, "Don't waste your
time thanking me," don't believe it! When someone makes a contribution to an organization, they deserve recognition and thanks. It must be
done tastefully and *quickly* once the pledge or gift is received. Just as
they want to belong, they want to be thanked. For the most part, the only
real payoff for donors in most organizations is this recognition and
thanks. It should never be treated routinely or casually. In most cases,
the thank you should be tangible—although it need not be expensive.

It is helpful to develop an attitude of donor cultivation on a year-
round basis. Existing donors must never be taken for granted. They
must continue to get newsletters, reports, invitations to activities, and
recognition throughout the year. A common complaint of most donors
is "the only time I hear from you is when you want money." Financial
commitment to the organization is enhanced when the donor feels that
he or she is personally responsible for some of the successful programs
provided by your organization. Therefore, keeping in touch with past
donors and educating potential donors must be systematic and pro-
grammed into your ongoing activities.

10. Communicate Action
and Success to Your Donors

A written brochure, often called the case statement, should help the
prospect feel that the organization is committed in a dynamic and
effective way to those values he or she has. People like to feel that their
contribution is used to help others. They like to support programs that
are new, expanding, and innovative. The case statement should be
simple, direct, action-oriented, and only long enough to create realism in
the mind of the reader. Ask yourself the question, "Why should I invest
in this organization?" Develop your written story from the perspective of
the potential donor. Most prospects have many opportunities to support

causes. Why your organization? Seek professional help if necessary, but make sure your copy creates mental images of success, action, and the prospects for a better tomorrow.

Further, since the case statement is left with the donor after solicitation is made, it becomes an ongoing communication tool that has value to the organization beyond the purposes of the campaign. While case statements by themselves do not raise money, they do provide valuable education for the prospect. Even though a prospect may say no to a particular solicitation, his or her education about the activities of the organization has been enhanced through the case statement, and a future request for support may be successful.

Notes

1. Virginia Ann Hodgkinson and Murray S. Weitzman, *The Charitable Behavior of Americans: Findings from a National Survey*, Independent Sector, Washington, D.C., 1985, p. 53.

PART 2

The Annual Fund-Raising Campaign

The foundation for any organization that wants to raise money over the long run is the annual campaign. Organizing and conducting an annual campaign gives your organization the credibility and strength it needs to successfully operate year after year. The techniques discussed in Chapters 4 and 5 will give you an understanding of the basic elements of conducting a campaign for support each year.

4
Organizing for the Campaign

Historically, many organizations have started as a result of a governmental grant, a single contributor, or citizen response to a specific problem. The new organization operates for a period of time on the proceeds of the initial money, providing services roughly equal to the dollars available. As time passes, the initial money is expended or the organization expands its services beyond the resources available.

At this point, the volunteer board is faced with the reality of the need to annually secure sufficient financial support to operate the organization for a fiscal year. By this time, it is not unusual for the organization to have several sources of income, including governmental grants and contracts, contributions by board members and active volunteers within the organization, and, in some organizations, fees for services paid by program participants. Other organizations may have income from activities, fund-raising dinners, and walkathons or other special events. However, even with several sources of income, the organization is faced with the reality of maintaining an ensured annual flow of income if the organization is to operate efficiently and effectively. The ultimate question is, how do we secure adequate financial support to operate our organization each year? The answer, with rare exceptions, is an annual fund-raising campaign.

The Campaign Concept

Annual fund-raising drives operated by most organizations are built on the campaign concept. The campaign concept evolved over many years and may have been influenced by the military. A military campaign has an objective that is reached with a given amount of resources in a given amount of time while overcoming obstacles or opposition. Accurate planning, training, and execution of the battle plan lead to either victory or defeat. Just as military campaigns do not operate in a static environment and must be flexible to adjust to changing conditions, the annual fund-raising campaign must follow similar principles to be successful.

In its simplest form, the campaign is a process whereby volunteer solicitors are recruited, trained, and motivated to make individual contacts seeking contributions by a specific target date.

In addition to recruiting and training volunteer solicitors, a successful campaign involves holding regular report meetings to ensure attention to deadlines and obtaining as much publicity as possible to recognize performance and make the constituency aware of the campaign. Ultimately, a victory meeting is held to celebrate successful attainment of the objective—a dollar goal in cash or pledges.

How It Began

The campaign concept for nonprofit organizations grew out of the work of two YMCA professional staff members, Lyman L. Pierce and Charles S. Ward, in the late 1890s. They were frustrated because fund raising took so much time away from their programs. Tired of living "hand-to-mouth" on small donations throughout the year while struggling to provide service to their constituency, these early pioneers, even though they worked somewhat independently of each other, developed fund-raising techniques that formed the basis of the now generally accepted campaign concept.[1]

A Widely Recognized Model

These campaign techniques, developed and refined by Pierce and Ward and influenced by dozens of others, can be observed today in almost all communities across America. One example is the annual United Way campaign. This campaign is launched with a public kickoff designed to generate a lot of public information about the campaign and its objectives. Initiating such publicity also forces the campaign leadership to recruit and train solicitors prior to kickoff, so that the actual campaign can begin on a specific date.

Once the campaign is off and running, United Way holds a series of report meetings to recognize performance, motivate campaign solicitors, and keep the public informed of the campaign success. Techniques such as displays of thermometers inching toward 100 percent or large clocks showing elapsed time toward the target date for completion are still utilized today in many communities just as they were in the early YMCA campaigns of Ward, Pierce, and others.

Six Fundamental Elements

All campaigns involve six fundamental elements:

1. A given time frame
2. A specific dollar goal
3. Volunteer solicitors
4. Regular report meetings
5. A public campaign kickoff
6. A victory celebration

All of these elements are applicable to any organization seeking to set up an annual campaign.

Campaign Volunteer Leadership

Strong volunteer leadership is the essential for success. While staff may do much of the work in planning and training, fund raising ultimately succeeds because committed, knowledgeable, and dedicated community leaders are willing to contribute their time and effort on behalf of the organization. Therefore, the recruitment of the general chairperson, a common title used in annual campaigns, must be approached carefully. With the possible exception of the recruitment of your organization's volunteer president or chairperson, there is no other position recruited during the course of the year that is more important. Since the operating funds for the organization are donated during this annual campaign, it is crucial for the top leadership to be the very best available.

The Steering Committee Functions

Once the general chairperson is recruited and committed, his or her first responsibility is to become personally involved in recruiting and organizing a campaign steering committee. While the size and makeup of this committee may be tailored to the specific organization involved, there are some fundamental functions that must be accomplished. In most cases, each function should have a volunteer chairperson and committee in place early in the campaign.

Six Basic Functions

The basic functions performed by subcommittees of the steering committee require a group of volunteers assigned as follows:

1. *The audit committee.*   Responsible for collecting, counting, and certifying to the board and to the public at large that the cash and pledges received have been properly handled and accounted for

2. *The training committee.*   Responsible for instructing all campaign workers in solicitation and reporting techniques used during the course of the campaign

3. *The prospects/rating committee.*   Responsible for identifying prospective donors and rating such donors as to the amount of their potential contribution

4. *The facilities committee.* Responsible for providing adequate meeting facilities for training and report meetings

5. *The communications committee.*   Responsible for media relationships and campaign literature

6. *The solicitation committee.*   Responsible for recruiting sufficient campaign solicitors to contact all prospects identified for solicitation in the campaign

Who Are We Going to Solicit?

The number of individuals identified as potential financial supporters of the organization becomes the initial controlling factor in developing the campaign organization. You cannot build your steering committee until you know how many people you want to solicit.

Your Natural Constituency

Some organizations have a natural constituency through membership or past activity with the organization. Others seek a much broader base of support from individuals in the community who may or may not have had any previous exposure to the organization. For example, Boy Scout Councils most often have a constituency base composed of adult volunteer leaders and the parents of members. This constituency base can be expanded easily through identifying "alumni"—adults who were Scouts as youngsters.

On the other hand, the local chapter of the USO has a relatively small natural constituency as compared to the large number of people they serve. Its most natural constituency, in addition to board members, is the military personnel it has helped. Only rarely would it have any records with good addresses, and then most would be living in other parts of the country. Therefore, beyond its board, the only natural prospect list the organization has would be the names of people who have helped provide service by serving as volunteers. Given this situation, the local chapter of a USO would be seeking a broader base of prospects from the public at large, who may or may not have participated in or received services from the USO.

Relative Size of the Constituency

There are certain cultural and geographic realities that also must be faced by some organizations. While some organizations are national in scope and may have a nationwide constituency, most usually have a geographic limitation based on services provided to a particular community, city, or region.

Possible Constraints

Some organizations, through their participation in local United Way campaigns, may be further restricted in whom they may contact, based on agreements with the United Way. Others may be further restricted through religious or cultural influences that may dictate the type of person who would be their most likely prospect.

Determining the Number of Solicitors Needed

Once the organization has an identified list of prospects by name, address, and perhaps phone number, it is easy to determine the number of solicitors needed. Fund-raising literature through the years has had different suggestions, but one solicitor contacting five prospects probably is a fairly standard measure for developing a campaign organizational structure. This is often referred to as the *rule of five*.

Experience has shown that it is reasonable to expect an individual solicitor to make five personal calls on prospects. Having to make more than five calls results in procrastination. It may also lead to telephone or mail contacts instead of person-to-person contacts. It is a rare solicitor who will make 10 or 15 personal contacts, no matter how committed he or she is to the objectives of the organization. It is also unlikely that any organization, no matter how strong, will recruit and train enough solicitors to enable them to make fewer than five contacts each.

Rule of Five

If an organization has a prospect list of 1000 prospects, using the rule of five, divide 1000 by 5. The result shows that the organization must recruit, train, and motivate 200 individual solicitors. Your natural constituency, if you have one, becomes the best source of campaign solicitors. If you have no natural constituency, you may be forced to develop a prospect list. Almost anyone can be a prospect for solicitation. A person who is a prospect for solicitation is also a prospect for help as a solicitor. In some instances, even relatively low-income recipients of service can and should be solicited in annual campaigns. Obviously, some prospects are capable of giving more money than others; therefore, prospects must be rated as to their financial capability. Figure 4.1 shows how a campaign seeking to see 625 prospects and requiring 125 solicitors might be organized.

I cannot overemphasize the importance of recruiting and training top-quality leadership. Figure 4.2 illustrates graphically what will happen if you recruit a volunteer that fails to complete the calls on the five prospects. If just one solicitor per captain fails to make calls, you will lose 125 potential donations. Twenty percent of your prospects will not be asked for a gift!

To keep this from happening, recruit good leadership, provide each person with good training on how to do the job, and make sure that there is good personal follow-up by volunteer leadership throughout the campaign.

Large Campaigns

When you are faced with soliciting several thousand probable donors, you need to subdivide your campaign. The rule of five still works. You will find it helpful to look for natural suborganization groups within

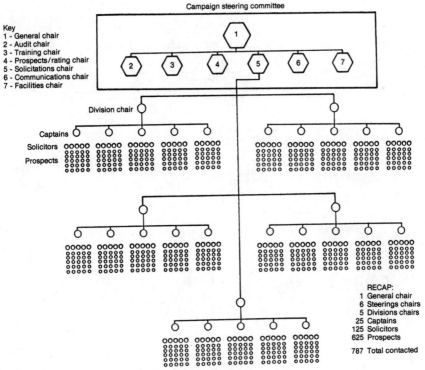

Figure 4.1 Campaign steering committee organization chart

your prospect base. Use your board and staff as one subunit within your campaign. Appoint a solicitation chairperson for the board and one for

the staff. If the board is large, divide the names by five and recruit captains for solicitation. Five captains soliciting five board members will cover a board of 25 members.

You can take your previous donors and divide these prospects into giving levels. Have a leadership gifts division, soliciting donors for $500 or more and, if necessary, a special gifts division seeking gifts above $100 but below $500. If you use gift clubs, divide your campaign along these support levels.

You may find it better to divide along geographic boundaries such as neighborhoods, cities, and counties. Regardless of the suborganizational concept that you use, follow the rule of five in recruiting solicitors. The initial solicitation chairperson should recruit five suborganizational leaders. If you need to stretch to six or seven, that will work, but at eight, add a vice chairperson, and he or she and the solicitation chairperson will each recruit four people.

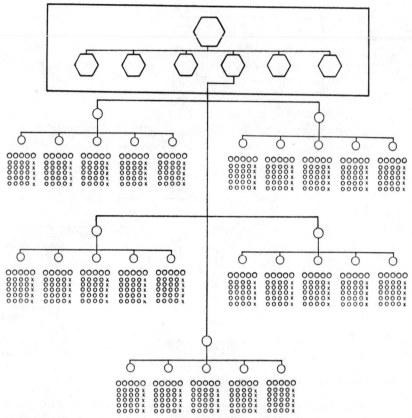

Figure 4.2 Results of nonperformance by a single solicitor in each team

The same principle holds for all functions in the campaign. For example, if you are using geographic divisions, the audit chairperson could have an audit chairperson from each subunit on the audit committee.

Prospect Rating and Evaluation

Embarrassment or reluctance may be the initial response of volunteers when asked to rate prospects. Therefore, it is important to understand why as well as how prospects are rated. Experience gained in past campaigns has shown that individuals, with rare exceptions, when asked for a gift will give the amount requested or less, not more. It is important that the person asking for the gift already be a contributor at about the same level as the prospect. In other words, don't ask a campaign worker who makes an annual contribution of $100 to solicit prospects who at best may only contribute $10. Without a rating system, it's quite possible to misuse highly effective and committed campaign workers to secure five gifts at a $10 level when they could have secured five gifts at a $100 level. Carefully matching solicitor to prospect could provide a net increase of $450 to the organization's annual operating funds.

Use Volunteers to Rate

In developing a prospects and ratings program, it is important for a group of volunteers to be involved who have some general knowledge of the type of people the organization seeks for its prospect list. There is no special formula for establishing potential giving. Studies done by the Internal Revenue Service show a fairly consistent giving pattern by individuals filing tax returns with itemized deductions. This very large group of citizens annually gives to charitable organizations approximately 2 percent of their income. This percentage has held fairly constant over the past 20 years or more. However, this factor is useless unless you know the specific income of the potential prospect. Even if you know the income of the individual, a 2 percent factor would be misleading, as it is an average drawn from millions of individual returns. The individual you are planning to solicit may normally give below the average or way above it.

Volunteers can fairly accurately estimate the approximate income levels of people they know from observation of life-style, residence, and job responsibilities. The educated guess will be accurate enough for the purposes of prospect rating, and little effort needs to be done on most of your prospects beyond this volunteer estimate, except in those cases where you will be seeking an extremely large gift.

Ask the Right Question

The basic question for the committee to ask itself is, "If this person had sufficient knowledge of our organization's work and was sufficiently motivated by our campaign solicitor, how much could he or she give?" Following this approach will more likely result in each prospect being properly evaluated and rated. Do not create too many potential giving levels. Start with a low range of $50 or less, then a midstep of $51 to $99, and a step of $100, and maybe a step or two more, if needed in your organization.

Be Careful of Giving History

Another technique is to review the giving history of each prospect, if one is available. This can be a trap, however, since some prospects may have historically given $10 per year because no one asked the appropriate question, "How much can he or she give?" It is probably best to have knowledgeable staff prescreen prospects, reviewing contribution records and noting those instances where, in staff judgment, an individual with a lower giving history can be upgraded to a higher giving level if properly motivated. The prospects and rating committee can review these suggestions, placing the appropriate rating on each prospect. When in doubt, rate up to a higher level.

The Mechanics of Rating Prospects

Many campaign organizations use what is commonly referred to as a *flatlist*, which is simply an alphabetized list of potential prospects with a series of columns to the right of the name where committee members can note a suggested rating. Once a small group of volunteers has independently reviewed the list, simply add these estimates and determine an average, rounding up to the categories already established. For example, if a person has an average rating of $88, round up to $100 for the campaign prospect file. This technique works reasonably well, even with prospect lists in large organizations where individuals are not known personally by members of the committee. Their names are recognized because of their participation in community or neighborhood organizations.

Rating Large Contributors.   For larger potential contributors, there probably needs to be a good bit of discussion among members of the committee to ensure that the prospect is rated at the correct level. When in doubt, rate at least one level higher than you might otherwise assign.

Remember, people rarely give more than you ask.   Many organizations find it helpful to translate financial evaluations to code letters which are then transferred to prospect cards in order to assist the solicitor in asking for an appropriate gift, without the potential embarrassment of disclosing someone's evaluation of potential giving capacity. For example, prospects rated at $1000 and above might be coded "A"; those between $750 and $999, "B"; those from $500 to $749, "C"; etc. Such a coding plan makes it relatively easy to provide suitable prospect cards to campaign solicitors.

Flatlists Help Control Your Campaign.   Flatlists (Figure 4.3), normally 8 ½ × 11 sheets of paper with alphabetized names, are also an important control mechanism. They provide a column to note which campaign solicitor has which prospect card, as well as a column to record the amount of the gift when received. Sometimes, certain other comments that are important for follow-up are also noted. Many organizations will either make carbon copies of the flatlist when it's typed or photocopy the flatlist and utilize it in a master control book, which is maintained in the permanent financial records of the organization. Additional copies may be provided to key staff and volunteers who perform supervisory roles in the campaign. With the availability of computer technology today, it isn't unusual for an organization to have the capacity of printing its prospect list on flatlists and later on prospect

Annual Campaign Flatlist			
Campaign level: _____ Date _____			
Division _____ Captain _____			
Name	Address	Gift	Solicitor

Figure 4.3 Annual campaign flatlist

cards. You do not need a computer to keep good campaign records, but having a good program and computer will make accurate information easily retrievable. If this capacity is available, use it.

The Campaign Pledge Card.   Prospect names are transferred from the flatlist or cards you have been using onto a pledge card. This card is a fundamental tool in annual campaigns, capital campaigns, and mail campaigns. The card should have a space for the name, address, and, if available, telephone number, as well as the evaluation amount or code. Some organizations even provide information on the card that allows the solicitor to know the date and amount of the last gift. As in all fund-raising activities, it is extremely important that the individual's-name be spelled correctly and that a full name is listed. Further, many prospect cards today become permanent records of the campaign. They provide a place for the individual's signature, indicating the amount of the pledge or gift. A place to designate whatever billing cycle the contributor desires is very helpful. More and more organizations are making it possible to pay a pledge through the use of a bank credit card. If this method is used, the pledge card would have a place for the contributor to add the information needed for your organization to collect from the issuer of the credit card. If you are going to use bank credit cards for payment of pledges, it is a good idea to discuss this with your bank to ensure that you have all of the information necessary to collect the pledge from the credit card issuer.

You can use a perforated tab on the pledge card that allows the solicitor to provide a written receipt. Additionally, it's very important to have the pledge card clearly state to whom the check should be made payable and to note that the gift is tax deductible. Large organizations find it effective to design their cards so that the names can be printed by computer, and some organizations go so far as to add individual identification numbers to cards so that they can track their progress during the course of the campaign. See Figure 4.4 for a sample of a pledge card incorporating most of the elements listed.

Setting the Campaign Goal

Setting a campaign goal is important, but often misunderstood. Some people assume that the campaign goal is simply a percentage increase over the amount raised the past year. Others assume that it is simply the difference between the total dollars needed for operating expense for the year, less other anticipated income. Both of these are simplistic and incomplete approaches to goal setting for campaigns.

Figure 4.4 Sample pledge card (*Courtesy of the Atlanta Area Council, Boy Scouts of America.*)

Set Your Goal with Care

With rare exceptions, most organizations tend to increase the amount of contributed dollars received on an incremental basis each year. In other words, there is some truth to the fact that track records for organizations tend to show trend lines of percentage increases on an annual basis.

Analysis of your organization's annual campaign success for the past 4 or 5 years will usually show a fairly consistent growth pattern. It is important to know this information. For example, if you have experienced an annual campaign growth of 8 to 10 percent over the past 5 years, to project a 100 percent increase in campaign goal over the previous year is unrealistic—unless some new element has entered the picture in developing the campaign. While it is possible for an organization to double its contributions in 1 year, it probably would not happen without new and exciting campaign leadership, additional reasons for approaching contributors, improved publicity, and, most of all, a dramatic increase in the number of active individuals involved in soliciting contributions.

It is also naive to simply fill in an amount needed to balance the budget in setting a campaign goal if such a goal is unrealistic in terms of historical performance. Setting an unattainable goal demoralizes volunteer solicitors and negates part of the campaign concept—the drive for victory. Likewise, a goal too quickly reached often leads to solicitors not calling on their assigned prospects.

Can You Set the Goal Too High?

Another debate is the relationship between the campaign goal and success of the campaign. Some argue that a high goal, if it's not attained, causes volunteers to work harder and reach higher levels of giving than they might obtain otherwise. The counterargument declares that volunteers want most of all to feel successful. Establishing a goal that cannot be reached within a reasonable period of time leads to disappointment, not success. Therefore, it is strongly recommended that the campaign goal be realistic and attainable as well as challenging.

Set a Contributor Goal As Well

In addition to setting a dollar goal, it is helpful to establish goals for contacting potential contributors. Since we know that people give to people and the amount contributed dramatically improves with face-to-face contact, it is important to set goals to expand the prospect base so that you are forced to look for new prospects, rather than continuing to deal with last year's givers. Setting contributor goals makes it possible to motivate campaign workers to solicit contacts even when they receive less than the requested amount. Even when the gift is smaller than requested, it is a gift, and it may be renewed and in many cases increased in future years. Having a large number of contributors often impresses other funding sources such as United Way, foundations, and corporations. It also reflects to a potential donor widespread community commitment to the organization.

Subunit Goals May Help

Large organizations also find it helpful to divide all of the above goals into suborganizational goals. For example, a Scout Council might have a councilwide goal for dollars, prospects, and contributors. In turn, it might subdivide these goals into geographic territories or districts. This is a very effective way of providing the volunteer leadership challenges for their own motivation and recognition.

Other organizations may subdivide into chapters, neighborhood units, or service groups. If the organization's constituency is served by geographic or service categories, it will often strengthen the campaign to utilize this natural organizational trait in the campaign.

The Campaign Schedule

How Much Time Does a Campaign Take?

Organizations with good records in conducting annual fund-raising campaigns usually have a well-established annual cycle. They start next year's campaign within a few days of completion of the current campaign. You could say that it takes a year to conduct a campaign—if you include the postcampaign evaluation from the previous year, followed by the planning, recruiting, and training process for campaign leadership during the coming year, the campaign itself, and then appropriate follow-up and record keeping at the conclusion of the campaign.

Realistically, most volunteers will be involved for a fairly short and concentrated period of time. From kickoff to victory meeting, the norm would be more like 4 to 8 weeks. Since most of us are guilty of a certain amount of procrastination, fund raisers learned years ago that it is important to start the campaign, provide solicitation cards for campaign volunteers, and set a target date that will require the solicitors to make their contacts at the earliest possible moment. Within reason, the tighter the schedule the better. A lot depends on the size of the campaign, the number of people involved, the type of leadership, and perhaps some consideration of geography. For instance, an organization conducting a campaign over a large territory has to coordinate the efforts of a number of smaller neighborhood or community campaigns within the area. This adds several more meetings for key campaign leadership and staff. It may require several training and kickoff sessions in different locations. These additional meetings will lengthen the campaign.

When to Conduct Your Campaign

There are two seasons during the year in which campaigns utilizing face-to-face solicitation should be avoided. Because of traditions and the psychology of the American culture, it seems that from mid-November through the beginning of January, our attention is turned to religious activities, vacations, and "the close of business." Campaigns attempted during this time do not receive enough attention from campaign solicitors to ensure success.

Campaigns during June, July, and August, when much of America considers itself on vacation, are tough, and should normally be avoided.

If your organization participates in a United Way campaign, you may be restricted from conducting a campaign during the fall season, when most annual United Way drives are conducted.

Thus, most organizations that seek broad-based community support find it best to conduct their annual campaign sometime between January and May.

Educational Institutions. Universities, colleges, and private schools find that the fall is a prime season for the start of their annual alumni campaigns. These institutions have no conflict with United Way since they are contacting only their own graduates and their campaigns do not affect the community at large. The early part of the new year becomes the follow-up phase of the campaign. Most of these organizations follow a fiscal year from July 1 to June 30, making it important for them to seek funding early in their fiscal years.

In each of these examples we are talking about the period of the actual solicitation process. The period for planning, recruiting, training, and development of campaign personnel and volunteers precedes this phase of the campaign.

Develop a Master Plan

For staff and key volunteers, a plan is needed that is even more comprehensive. Start it with a thorough review and analysis of the campaign results from the previous year. Also review campaign and training materials with an eye toward improvement. Provide sufficient time for the development of campaign literature and ordering of office supplies to support the campaign organization. Establish tentative dates for the various meetings and other activities needed in the campaign. It should include start-up and completion dates for each function of the campaign.

The Campaign Calendar.   No campaign is likely to succeed without a master calendar and a campaign schedule that includes the smallest details that must be accomplished. Your calendar should include target dates or deadlines for recruiting the general campaign chairperson, the campaign steering committee, and the campaign solicitors, as well as dates for training campaign workers and the kickoff, report, and victory meetings.

Suborganization Calendars.   Once this master calendar is in place, a series of additional calendars would grow out of the master calendar. These would include a calendar for the general campaign chairperson and the campaign steering committee which would key on recruiting deadlines, kickoff meetings, report meetings, and victory meetings, in each case allowing adequate time for recruiting and training the necessary personnel to conduct the campaign.

If the organization's campaign is divided into subgroups as noted earlier, such groups would also have calendars that would fit into the master plan and would be an outgrowth of events scheduled for the campaign steering committee. For example, an area campaign chairperson would have a calendar customized for his or her particular area of responsibility, listing recruiting deadlines, training dates, and kickoff events. Figure 4.5 outlines the key elements in a master calendar. Your calendar will need to be developed for your own campaign based on the organizational structure you will be using.

Calendar Coordination. It is absolutely essential that all of these calendars be coordinated so that each volunteer involved has an opportunity to complete his or her assigned task prior to the campaign organization taking the next step. For example, the deadline for recruiting area campaign chairpersons by the general campaign chairperson should be met prior to the date established for training those area chairpersons.

Campaign Discipline. The master calendar with its subdivisions is the basic document that ensures campaign discipline. Your annual campaign is keyed toward a public kickoff and specific completion date, during which time solicitations are made and you reach your objectives in dollars, prospect contacts, and donors. Without the discipline created by deadlines, the campaign ceases to be an annual campaign and becomes instead an annual giving plan. If this happens, volunteers grow weary of constantly worrying about contributions to keep your organization running, and much volunteer energy is siphoned *away* from program delivery *toward* fund-raising activities. Few, if any, volunteers will stay actively involved in your campaign if it seems to have no end.

There is an old joke in sports circles that has a clear message for campaigners. At the conclusion of the game, the losing coach was asked by a reporter why the team had lost. The coach responded that the team would have won if the game had lasted a few minutes longer because the players were "finally getting the hang of it." Of course, that's not how the score is kept. If you can't score points in the allotted time, you don't win.

Too many annual campaigns are conducted with the attitude that the time frame for the campaign will be extended until all the contacts are made and all the money is raised. While on rare occasions a campaign may be extended for a week or two when victory is in sight, campaigns without a firm completion date rarely, if ever, succeed. In those cases where the volunteers reach the goal early, if the campaign included contributor goals as well as dollar goals, the campaign leadership can often increase the dollar goal and reach higher levels of success.

Training Campaign Leadership

If a campaign chairperson follows good recruiting techniques, volunteers can be found to help. Although volunteers rarely make a commitment with the

BASIC ELEMENTS IN AN ANNUAL CAMPAIGN

July	• Review last year's results.
	• Improve support material as needed.
	• Develop new case statement.
	• Establish tentative objectives for dollars and prospects.
August	• Identify potential volunteer leadership.
	• Establish campaign organization structure (levels of giving, geographic groups).
	• Recruit general chairperson.
September	• Recruit steering committee.
	• Train steering committee.
	• Recruit needed membership on functional committees.
	• Hold a training session for staff and support personnel.
October	• Develop promotional and communication materials.
	• Secure needed meeting facilities.
	• Finalize goals for dollars and prospects.
	• Start prospect identification and evaluation.
November	• Conduct campaign for board and staff.
	• Training for volunteer leadership at area and gift levels.
	• Begin recruiting volunteer solicitors for area and gift levels.
	• Start weekly campaign newsletter.
	• Complete prospect identification and evaluation.
December	• Train volunteers at area and gift club levels.
	• Start major gifts solicitation calls.
January	• Complete recruitment of all captains.
	• Train all captains.
	• Finish recruiting campaign solicitors.
	• Finish major gifts solicitation calls.
February	• Hold kickoff/orientation meeting for general campaign.
	• Report meeting 1.
	• Report meeting 2.
	• Report meeting 3.
	• Report meeting 4.
March	• Victory meeting.
	• Campaign clean-up.
	• Recognition/thanks to volunteer leadership.

Figure 4.5 Basic elements in an annual campaign

idea of failure, they may plow ahead in the wrong direction, without proper guidance. Therefore, training and orientation of volunteers in campaign plans and procedures are of crucial importance to success.

Follow the Plan

The very concept of a campaign plan as discussed earlier makes it vitally important that all volunteers understand and then carefully follow the plan. This creates quite a challenge for staff and key campaign leadership. Volunteers will often shortcut or alter their responsibilities in the campaign because of uneasiness, confusion, or downright stubbornness. We know, for example, that face-to-face solicitation is the proven way to solicit financial contributions. But asking someone directly for money is a task that many people find difficult to face up to. Instead, they will be quick to mail a prospect card to an individual, call the person on the phone, or in some other way do less than what was expected.

In addition, some campaign leaders, particularly at lower levels, find it difficult to recruit. Instead of recruiting sufficient campaign solicitors to provide a ratio of 1 solicitor for each 5 prospects, they may independently decide to give each solicitor 10 or more cards, with a resulting reduction in success. The point is simply this: If you expect volunteers to follow your plan, they must *understand* the plan and the role they play in it, and they must be committed to the successful attainment of the campaign goal. In addition, they need to understand why the organization needs money, how to conduct an effective solicitation call, and how to respond to questions.

Remember the advice we have all heard many times: when confused or in doubt, follow the directions! This is a critical principle in conducting good campaigns.

What Volunteers Must Know

While actual training outlines must be customized, based on your organization and its programs, the fundamentals remain the same. Volunteers must be given sufficient information about the programs and services of the organization to be able to communicate effectively about what the organization does, why it performs this service, and what the benefits are to the community. In short, they must understand the functions of the organization and believe its benefits are worth their personal financial investment, as well as their time in soliciting others.

Help Volunteers Feel Excitement

Communicating the right amount of information about your organization is more difficult than it seems. Most organizations deliver outstanding services and programs for participants, but unless the campaign volunteer has actually experienced or assisted in delivering this service, it's difficult for that person to understand the impact of such a service. An organization working with blind children, for example, has a number of counselors who can tell dramatic stories about youngsters learning to cope with their blindness. Yet, communicating how exciting this is to a solicitor or a potential prospect is difficult. To help in this process, slide presentations, visits to service facilities, success stories shared by caseworkers, etc., should be a part of volunteer training.

Tell Volunteers Why You Need Money

Beyond understanding the mission and the services of your organization, volunteers must understand how the organization is financed and why it needs contributions. While this does not need to be the kind of in-depth financial understanding a member of your board might have, volunteers need to understand your major sources of income and some specifics on how that money is spent. You will find it helpful to develop campaign materials with illustrations that help readers visualize where the money comes from and how it's spent. Pie charts or graphs are effective ways to show the allocation of your resources to your services and their related costs. (See Figure 4.6.) You may also find it useful to develop a small brochure on the 10 questions most often asked by prospects and the answers to those questions.

Personal Commitment

At the conclusion of the volunteer training program, which probably lasts a minimum of 1 to 2 hours over and above visits to facilities (if visits are needed to help volunteers understand the work of your organization), it is important to give each participant an opportunity to make his or her personal pledge to the campaign. No one should solicit others without first having made his or her own personal commitment. The level of gift made by the volunteer at this meeting identifies which level prospects he or she will be asked to contact. An old saying among fund

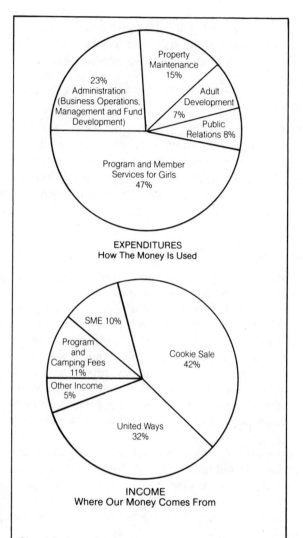

EXPENDITURES
How The Money Is Used

INCOME
Where Our Money Comes From

Please look carefully at these charts. You'll notice that our revenues come from five sources, and that of the three largest, two must remain at the same level in the coming year and the third — contributions from United Way — will actually drop. **So we are counting on our Sustaining Membership Enrollment (SME) to grow in 1985.**

Your participation through financial support is critically important to the continued success of the Girl Scout Council of Northwest Georgia. Working together, the adult volunteers, parents and friends of Girl Scouting can keep our program strong . . . so that **not one** *Girl must lose her opportunity to prepare for the future.*

Figure 4.6 Sample budget display (Courtesy of the Northwest Georgia Girl Scout Council.)

raisers says it all: "Ford dealers drive Fords." This principle is important because it not only makes it easier for the volunteer to solicit others, but it ensures that the volunteer is making a peer-to-peer solicitation.

Secure Board Support First

You will find it very helpful to be able to say at the beginning of a campaign that "100 percent of our board made a financial commitment to this year's campaign." While recognizing that not all board members would be rated for the same size gift, this is still a way to clearly indicate the strength of the organization through contributions of its individual members.

How to Make a Solicitation

Many organizations find it very helpful to conduct role-playing sessions on how to make a solicitation contact. Other organizations have developed film strips or slides showing how to make a personal solicitation. Whatever teaching method is chosen, the technique of making a person-to-person solicitation is an important part of a volunteer training program. Despite the training provided, people will do it in a way that is most comfortable to them. Therefore, it is extremely important that *the very best role model* is placed before them, so that personal modifications will be held to a minimum. Chapter 8 provides more detail on how to make a personal solicitation and includes an outline of a volunteer training/kickoff meeting.

Under normal circumstances, campaign solicitors will leave the training/kickoff meeting having selected their five cards for personal contact. If the training program is conducted effectively, volunteers will be at their highest level of motivation and more likely to make personal contacts within a day or two, if they have made their own personal commitment at that time.

Matching Prospects to Solicitors

Prospect Selection

There are probably several dozen ways to distribute prospect cards to solicitors, all the way from actual assignment by campaign leadership to random drawing for names. Depending on the size of the meeting and the number of people involved, one of the more effective methods is to allow each individual solicitor to review all the prospect cards, personally selecting those with whom the solicitor feels an affinity. This is as simple as laying out the prospect cards in alphabetical order, and asking solicitors to select five cards.

Variations.   An alternative that has proved successful is to have solicitors "draft" prospects by picking one name in rotation through the team until each member has five prospect cards.

Another variation of this form of prospect selection is to have the team captain and the five campaign workers he or she recruited work as a team in selecting cards. The team's job is done when all 25 contacts are made. Each team member is responsible for five cards, but if one volunteer fails to complete contacts, other team members can fill in, thus improving chances of getting all 25 contacts made during the campaign time frame.

Keep Up with the Cards

Once the solicitor makes his or her own selection, a record is left with the campaign leadership as to which cards the individual solicitor has agreed to call on. This can be done with a report card or a perforated stub on the original prospect card.

Separate Solicitors by Giving Levels

Peer-to-peer solicitation is also enhanced if the training/kickoff meetings can be subdivided so that when solicitors are choosing prospects, the group is selecting prospects rated at the same level. In other words, don't mix $100 prospect cards in with $50 prospect cards.

What to Do about Unassigned Cards

Since we are talking about the principles of involving volunteers in raising money, the inevitable question will come up on what happens to cards that weren't selected at the meeting. If the recruiting standards have been maintained (one to five), and if 100% of the solicitors are in attendance, all the cards should have been selected. Unfortunately, real world experience shows that this is rarely the case.

Have a Backup Plan Ready.   Therefore, a backup plan must be inplace. Several alternatives can be considered. *First,* the team captains can meet at the conclusion of the meeting and draw cards for their campaign workers who could not attend. *Second,* a follow-up training/kickoff meeting for those who weren't in attendance can be scheduled, so that they can select their cards from those remaining. *Third,* cards can be assigned based on some criterion that seems logical, such as residence, place of employment, etc.

Your Best Alternative.   Caution should be exercised in any alternative plan. Active promotion of the initial training/kickoff meeting with the objective of 100% attendance is worth the effort. The dynamic of the meeting is important. Being in a group where those attending are all striving for the same goal reinforces commitment and is an important success factor. A follow-up meeting to motivate those who could not attend is probably the best alternative.

Teamwork may be an overused term, but it is seldom an overused factor in successful campaigns. Creating that feeling of being "part of a team" will produce ongoing enthusiasm and a strong desire to "win." If volunteers do not participate in preparation activities, it is more difficult for them to catch the *feeling* of teamwork.

After the Calls Are Completed

An additional incentive to solicitors to make their calls is to ask for an "after-action" report. This is a simple report submitted with the pledge cards that have been signed. It asks the solicitor to reflect for a few moments and provide you with some valuable information that will help you do a better job in training solicitors in later campaigns, and just may give you some insights about how your prospects view your organization.

Keep the form simple. One page should do. Ask the following questions:

1. What questions were you asked?
2. What objections did any of the people you visited raise?
3. What positive comments did you hear from those you called on?
4. What negative comments did you pick up?
5. What suggestions do you have that would help us improve our campaign for next year?

While some solicitors will not fill out such a report, you will get some valuable feedback that will help you prepare your campaign material for the next campaign. It will also help you do a better job helping next year's solicitors prepare for their calls. It may also help you get an idea or two that you should educate your constituency about.

Notes

1. Scott M. Cutlip, *Fund Raising in the United States*, New Jersey, University Press, 1965, pp. 48–49, 158.

5
Special Aspects of the Annual Campaign

The Audit Function

The audit function in the annual fund-raising campaign is frequently seen as an administrative process, and therefore delegated to staff employees of the organization. This often happens because the volunteers involved in the annual fund-raising campaign fail to understand the importance of the audit function and tend to regard it as record keeping at best.

Four Basic Purposes

The audit function really has four essential purposes, (1) scorekeeping, (2) accounting and reporting, (3) financial disclosure, and (4) providing credibility and integrity. All are important to the long-term success of the organization and the operation of its annual fund-raising campaign.

Scorekeeping. First, and perhaps most obvious, the audit function becomes scorekeeping during the course of the campaign and helps keep the organization and its volunteer leadership aware of the progress of the campaign. If the organization has gone to the trouble of having a campaign goal expressed in dollars, it is important that regular reports be provided to the campaign leadership indicating progress toward that objective. Keeping score has become so much a part of the value system of American society that people expect reports indicating success toward the objective. When campaigns are running behind, there is often a reluctance to publish campaign reports to keep from embarrassing those volunteers who have not performed the assignments accepted. Having a chairperson and a group of volunteers assigned this responsibility as a part of the campaign steering committee ensures that this function is carried out in a timely and appropriate manner. This scorekeeping function becomes an additional element of campaign discipline discussed earlier.

Accounting and Reporting. The second purpose of the audit function is related to the responsibility all nonprofit organizations have to account accurately for and report on contributed dollars to donors and to the public at large. Donors have a right to expect that their money is properly recorded. Within the last several decades, a number of organizations have tarnished the image of fund raising because of extremely high fund-raising costs or poor handling of funds. Governing boards of nonprofit organizations have a fiduciary responsibility to donors and the public to make full disclosure about the financial affairs of the organization, including the cost of raising funds. It is rare for an individual donor to request copies of organization audits or other financial reports, because the vast majority of all nonprofit organizations have done a good job of accounting for their income and expenses and as a result have credibility in the minds of most people.

Financial Disclosure. The third purpose of the audit function may be a legal requirement. A number of states have passed laws requiring financial disclosure documents, audits, and the like be filed with the state annually, in order for the organization to maintain its right to publicly ask for donations. Failure to provide this information to state agencies can result in the loss of an organization's charter or certification. In some cases it may lead to some type of public warning that the organization is not meeting preestablished standards of performance in fund-raising techniques and costs. Additionally, some volunteer agencies have become "watchdogs," attempting to warn the public about organizations that do not meet minimal standards by their definition.

Credibility and Integrity. Perhaps the audit function's most important purpose of all is one that is often not understood by the vast majority of volunteers involved in helping raise money for their favorite organization. Integrity is a character attribute that is gained over time and lost quickly when even a hint of inappropriate behavior is suggested. Therefore, it is important for the organization to understand that the audit function is to help maintain the integrity of both staff and volunteers involved in raising money. When literally hundreds of people are handling cash, checks, or pledge cards during the course of a major fund-raising campaign, even individuals with no intention of misappropriating donated dollars can inadvertently lose, misplace, or forget contributed dollars—without some formal procedure established by the campaign steering committee to ensure that all pledge cards are accounted for and accuracy is verified.

Public accounting firms auditing the financial affairs of nonprofit organizations are required by the American Institute of Certified Public Accountants (AICPA) to review the accounting and auditing procedures of the annual drive just as they are charged with verifying other financial transactions of the organization. Without these procedures, therefore, an organization may not get an "unqualified audit," which can be devastating for an organization and in some cases can lead to loss of corporate charter or loss of Internal Revenue Service certification as a not-for-profit, tax-deductible entity.

Records and Reports

Campaign records are important because donors are individuals and expect to be treated as such. Therefore, the audit committee must ensure that accurate records including the correct spelling of names and addresses are a routine part of the campaign process. People who gave last year expect this year's campaign solicitors to know that information. Often the prospect will ask, "How much did I give last year?" Accurate records of previous donations are the best and initial source of prospects for the next campaign.

Another major responsibility for the audit committee is the development and issuing of periodic campaign reports. As noted earlier, periodic reports help keep score and become a motivating factor in the successful completion of the campaign. While some individuals may be embarrassed by lack of performance or success, regular reporting of campaign results to all volunteers involved in the annual campaign is an essential ingredient in a successful campaign.

Keep campaign reports simple to produce and understand. They need to indicate the name of the volunteer responsible for a segment of the campaign, the total number of prospects to be contacted, the total dollar goal, and the actual results to date. The reports need not be elaborate or difficult to produce. With the invention of photocopying machines, weekly campaign reports are easy to produce. At the start of the campaign, type the form showing the names of all individual solicitors and campaign leadership and the appropriate contributor and dollar goals. Columns showing results for the week can be filled in by hand and the report distributed to all campaign personnel. Figure 5.1

CAMPAIGN PROGRESS REPORT

REPORT #_____   AS OF:_____

NAME	DIVISION	TOTAL PROSPECTS	NUMBER GIFTS	%	$ GOAL	$ REPORTED	% GOAL	TEAM RECORD
								-100%
								-90%
								-80%
								-70%
								-60%
								50%

Figure 5.1. Campaign progress report

shows an example of one easy-to-produce campaign report. An added benefit of this type of report is the use of the reverse side as a newsletter offering congratulations, encouragement, or other information about the campaign to keep it moving. It might also carry a thermometer showing percent of success to date.

Receipts and Acknowledgments

With rapidly rising labor and postage costs, increasing concern and debate has developed in fund-raising circles about the necessity of acknowledging individual gifts. For very large campaigns collecting very small contributions, it may be economically impossible to receipt and acknowledge all individual gifts. However, for most organizations, the receipt and acknowledgment of gifts continues to be a worthwhile fund-raising cost. All cash gifts must be receipted. It may be satisfactory to state on pledge cards that the cancelled check will serve as the individual's receipt for tax purposes. However, even where a written receipt may seem redundant, it plays the important role of giving acknowledgment and a "thank you" to the donor. Obviously, at some modest giving levels this may be an inappropriate or inefficient use of funds, but the larger the gift the more important the acknowledgment.

Some organizations have attempted to deal with the issue of receipts and acknowledgments through use of thank you cards that are attached to the pledge card with perforations, allowing for signature by the solicitor at the time of the solicitation. This may not be an effective technique in some campaigns, but may be an important crutch for the solicitors who feel the need for some receipting process at the time of solicitation.

A more effective receipting process is a simple card noting the receipt number, the amount of the gift, and a thank you statement that can either be mailed in an envelope or as a postcard acknowledging the individual's gift.

Large Gift Acknowledgment. Special treatment is important for large givers. Depending on the size of the gift, there may be a series of acknowledgments. While all gifts may be important to the total success of the campaign, obviously substantial gifts deserve special attention. Whereas a $100 contributor might receive a thank you letter with receipt enclosed, a $1000 contributor might receive not only the normal thank you letter, but a special note from the campaign chairperson or board officer. These special letters need to be as personal as possible; a feeling of identity with the organization is an important motivating factor for donors. Printed receipts for tax purposes may be acceptable, but genuine thank you letters should be used for larger gifts.

Pledges and Billing

Seeking pledges instead of checks or cash increases the size of the gift. As the number of pledges increases, receipt and acknowledgment also becomes part of the billing process. If a pledge is made, acknowledgment can be a simple statement thanking the individual for the pledge and confirming for the record the amount of the pledge and the billing cycle requested by the donor. While it is very rare, it is not unknown for the spirit of competition to lead some campaign solicitors to alter a pledge card for reporting purposes. Confirming pledges will solve such a problem. Figure 5.2 is an example of a pledge confirmation that is effective in thanking the donor and confirming the pledge.

Donor Cultivation and Recognition

A Year-round Attitude

Donor cultivation is first and foremost an attitude. Volunteers involved in the work of your organization and its staff must recognize that the life blood of the organization is its donors. Just as the private enterprise company must develop a "satisfaction guaranteed attitude" as they deal with customers, so must a nonprofit organization treat its donors. If your organization is one where donors are also users of services, you must be doubly sure that its dealings with them have an open and positive tone.

This attitude is reflected in a number of ways. The careful attention to the spelling of names and correct addresses is fundamental. The understanding by staff and key volunteers that every conversation they have with friends, associates, and the public at large is an opportunity to share the story of your organization. Remember, contacts with donors outside of campaign time are equally important and must reflect care and appreciation for the support of the donor. Therefore, periodic reports to donors outside the time frame of the campaign keep important channels of communication open.

Thank You. . .

. . .for your financial commitment in support of our YMCA youth program. Such tangible "votes of confidence" are a source of encouragement and we pledge our continuing effort to fulfill the expectations you have of us.

If our records, as shown below, need any correction I will appreciate your calling it to my attention with a phone call or note.

Your total commitment: $_____

Payment received: $_____

Balance on commitment: $_____

_____

METRO ATLANTA YMCA
100 EDGEWOOD AVE., NE, SUITE 902, ATLANTA, GA 30303
588-9622

Figure 5.2. Pledge confirmation (Courtesy of the Metro Atlanta YMCA.)

Ongoing Research. Further, strong organizations keep up with what's happening within the community through careful reading of newspapers, including neighborhood newspapers, the business press, and even house organs published by major employers throughout the year. It is important to know, for example, that a potential donor has been actively involved as a volunteer in the community symphony, a local youth agency, or the United Way campaign. Such participation is a clear indication of the individual's willingness to support organizations with time and money. This information on donors and potential donors becomes very important in developing campaign leadership and in the evaluation of prospects for future campaigns.

Planned Promotion. Throughout the year, opportunities to demonstrate the program of the organization to potential donors should be planned and implemented. Board members and other volunteers should be encouraged and supported with printed material so that they find it easy to share the work of the organization with friends.

As noted earlier, acknowledgment and thanks for gifts is a routine part of good campaigning. This might be a letter signed by the organization's chief volunteer leader or the campaign chairperson. If the organization's annual campaign includes "membership," the thank-you might be a wallet-sized card identifying the donor as a member of the organization.

Tangible Recognition. Beyond this recognition, many organizations have found it very helpful to have a series of recognition plaques, certificates, or other mementos depending on the giving level. Many organizations use a "century club" plaque or certificate designating $100 contributions. Some organizations have successfully used plaques or certificates with places to affix small indicators of continued giving so that the plaque might be effective for 4 or 5 years. Beyond plaques there are such things as paperweights, lapel pins, or other tangible reminders to the donor of the appreciation of the organization.

Special Presentations. These recognition pieces can be presented publicly at board meetings of the organization or other public gatherings and reap additional benefits for the organization. Where there are a large group of contributors to receive recognition pieces, however, it is important that the recognition be delivered in a timely manner. Therefore, it may become difficult to present such awards at public gatherings. If this problem arises, it is probably better to mail or hand deliver the recognition piece in lieu of waiting for the donor to participate in some public activity. Some youth agencies have found it effective to have youth members of the agency deliver the recognition pieces to the homes or offices of large donors.

In addition to the actual presentation of some recognition piece, additional recognition of donors can be accomplished through listings of names and giving level in newsletters or annual reports of the organization. Colleges and universities are particularly fond of doing this, and often list the donor by giving level and by class group.

Are Recognition Pieces a Waste of Money? Sooner or later in any volunteer organization, someone will suggest that it is a waste of money to spend funds on recognition pieces for donors. These people are well meaning and have concluded that the donor really intends for the money to go toward program or delivery of service. However, while 1 person in 100 might have such a reaction, the other 99 are genuinely motivated by the recognition. Indeed, there is much evidence that volunteers will actually increase the amount of giving if it is tied to a larger, more attractive, or publicly visible recognition.

Some years ago, after a board meeting where a number of individuals were recognized with the presentation of "Patron" plaques in appreciation for the individual's donation of $500 to the annual campaign, a member of the board approached the author and asked why he had not received such a plaque. After checking the campaign records later, I told him that his gift to the current campaign was for $250. Whereupon, he mailed a check for an additional $250 and received his "Patron" plaque at the next board meeting.

Levels of Giving

There is not much doubt that levels of giving are appropriate for annual campaigns. Levels can be established by your organization based on local conditions. They are a motivating factor for many donors. Designations such as regular member, sustaining member, patron member, life member, are quite common, as are such terms as century club, presidents club, and founders circle. Giving levels are a clear indication that there are additional recognition benefits for donors based on increased contributions to the organization. Figure 5.3 shows the various giving levels used on the pledge card. This listing invites the donor to consider an increased gift by letting the person know that there are higher giving levels and recognition programs.

The Trap in Giving Levels. Establishing giving levels can become a problem because of inflation. During the forties and fifties, many organizations seeking to increase giving levels from the casual out-of-pocket cash response, established "buck-a-month club" levels seeking to move the $5 contributor to a $12 contributor. When initially established, these were dramatic increases in giving levels. However, in later years as

On The Way Up!!!

GSU PANTHER CLUB
1986 — 1987

☐ New Member
☐ Renewal

Name ______________________
Spouse's Name ______________________ Date ________
Home Address ______________________ Home Phone ________
City ____________ State ____________ Zip ________
Business/Or Occupation ______________________
Business Address ______________________ Bus. Phone ________

Your Pledge		Company's Matching Gift		Total Pledge	Paid Now
	+		=		

Please Bill Me: ☐ Annually ☐ Semi-Annually ☐ Quarterly 1985-1986 Gift $________

________ Membership Secured By
________ Member's Signature

Make Check Payable To: **GSU Athletic Association**

THE PANTHER CLUB
Georgia State University
University Plaza
(404) 658-2772

Membership Classification

- ☐ President's Society — Athletics ($1000 +)
- ☐ Phoenix Group — Athletics ($500 - $999)
- ☐ Ambassador Club — Athletics ($250 - $499)
- ☐ Centurian Club — Athletics ($100 - $249)
- ☐ Cub Level ($50 - $99)

OFFICE USE ONLY
Date ________
Amt ________
Comp ________
Alumni ________

Please send Panther Club information to the following people:

Name ______________________
Company ______________________
Address ______________________
City ____________ State ______ Zip ______
Phone (B) ____________ (R) ____________

Name ______________________
Company ______________________
Address ______________________
City ____________ State ______ Zip ______
Phone (B) ____________ (R) ____________

Please send me information on:

☐ Men's Basketball Season Tickets
☐ GSU Panther Celebrity Golf Tournament
☐ GSU Athletic Association Endowment Fund

GSU alumnus ______ Yes ______ No
______ Year ______________ degree

Figure 5.3. Pledge card with giving levels (Courtesy of the Georgia State University Athletic Association.)

inflation affected the economy, a $12 gift no longer seemed to be a substantial gift; yet contributors had been trained to give a "buck-a-month." In 1933, Clemson University started the IPTAY club, which stood for "I pay ten a year." The same problem ensued; today the IPTAY club is an important part of Clemson's athletic program, but it no longer stands for "I pay ten a year." Today it means "I pay thirty a year." Additional levels have been added to increase financial support of Clemson's athletic program.

Similarly, century clubs, after successful use in the early years, became a limit on giving for some organizations. In large measure, these limiting factors led to the increased use of higher and higher giving levels with different recognition programs.

Identifying the Donor's Gift with Service Delivery. Some organizations have found it helpful to identify the "cost of a unit of service." For example, if it cost the local Boy Scout Council $50 a year to provide the scouting program for each youngster enrolled, it is possible for contributors to sponsor one scout, two scouts, five scouts, and so on.

Hospitals often use the cost of patient care on a per day or procedure basis when requesting donations. Such techniques help establish giving levels in the mind of the donor, and may encourage increased giving from regular donors. Many donors apparently like to identify with a specific service or individual they helped by their donation.

Use of Membership Fees

The concept of the membership fee is a fairly complex one for general treatment. Some nonprofit organizations belong to national associations which require a national membership fee, and these fees are controlled by the national association. Other organizations are autonomous, and may choose to establish a membership fee as a source of raising operating funds. Since one of the primary motivating factors of positive donor response is affiliation with the organization and its objectives, the concept of membership is an important one in fund raising. Therefore, depending on the local or national criteria involved with a particular organization, in most cases it will be helpful for the annual campaign to include membership in the organization. This can be done with a special membership card, receipt of a special quarterly newsletter from the organization reporting on activities, and from time to time special invitations to donors to participate in activities of the organization as its guest. If a membership fee is established as a source of annual income, care must be exercised to ensure that the fee exceeds the cost of securing and servicing it.

However, be careful with membership fees! In some cases, donors may feel that by joining at some modest membership level, they have done all that they need to do to help the organization on an annual basis. If the membership fee is relatively low, the operating needs of the organization will be hard to secure.

Communicating Your Message

Even though the primary objective during the annual campaign is to recruit and train sufficient volunteer solicitors to personally ask prospects for a contribution, a campaign must be supported by good campaign literature designed to assist the work of the volunteers involved in the campaign. There are three basic pieces of campaign literature and almost unlimited options based on the size of the campaign, the message to be communicated, and the resources available for this support.

Basic Campaign Literature

The three essential elements are: 1) the pledge card, 2) case statement, and 3) the budget or financial statement.

The Pledge Card.   As noted in Chapter 4, the pledge card is important to the control and auditing functions of the campaign. It is also important in communicating the organization's message. The campaign or organization logo or slogan should be a part of the pledge card. Also, do not forget to include your organization's name. I have seen pledge cards that did not have the identity or name of the organization anywhere. If other campaign material is misplaced, the prospect may not remember what the gift is for. Figure 4.4 shows an example of a good pledge card. Yours need not look exactly like this one, but it should include all of the elements seen here.

The Case Statement.   The case statement is probably the most important piece of campaign literature and deserves careful attention and development. Basically, it is an attempt to put in writing a brief, clear statement that communicates the purpose, program, and financial needs of the organization. It really answers the question of why you are conducting the campaign. But more than that, it is a public statement that must stand alone without explanation or amplification, and should seek to create in the minds of the reader the excitement and accomplishment the donor can expect by supporting the work of the organization.

   The case statement should be written from the donor's point of view. The goal is to have the reader feel a sense of involvement or identity with your organization, and therefore the case statement must answer the questions the donor might have. It should clearly state what the work of the organization is and why it is important to the donor and the community. It should also be oriented toward the future. State what you will accomplish with financial support. The number of children in camp or the number of new clients served will help people feel they can help accomplish something they can feel good about. Finally, it should include an invitation to participate through a financial contribution to the organization.

The Financial Statement. The financial statement may be an additional page in the case statement or may be a separate piece. It is usually best to explain your sources of income and how you expend those funds in some graphic way. You have probably seen brochures with stacks of coins representing how the money is received and how it is used. Other variations include pie charts and segments of a dollar bill. The important message is to show that the donor's contribution provides direct services or benefits to those clients of the organization with which the donor wishes to identify. Helping pay the rent is not very exciting to most donors, but providing shelter and care for abused children is. Pictures of your organization's delivery of service enhances this statement and should be utilized when possible.

Add Additional Credibility. A further implication of this budget or financial statement relates to the financial integrity of the organization. Statements noting that the books of the organization are audited annually by a CPA, that the organization is a member of the local United Way, the Better Business Bureau, the Chamber of Commerce, etc., all give credibility to the financial affairs of the organization. One caution, however: too much budget detail is probably more confusing than helpful. This is not to imply that you should attempt to hide any information; but you should accurately communicate how the organization receives and spends its annual income. Figure 5.4 illustrates a campaign brochure displaying the kind of information that is important in the campaign.

The names of key campaign and organization leadership should be included in both the case statement and the budget display if it is separate from the case statement.

Campaign Support Material. Additional campaign literature might include such things as a list of projects that a donor may personally identify with and provide money to support. Examples of this are (1) the cost of furnishing a hospital room, (2) sending one needy youngster to camp for a week, (3) providing a medical examination, or (4) 1 hour of counseling time.

Also integrated into the campaign literature are certain other support documents, including a report envelope, instructions for campaign solicitors, and newsletters and reports on campaign progress. The goal is to ensure that all printed material related to the campaign is identified as such. Therefore a campaign logo or slogan appearing on all campaign literature helps those who use this printed material recognize that this is a part of the campaign process. If you use similar graphics from one year to the next, be sure to date the material. Your volunteers need the

DID YOU KNOW...

- Over 30% of our youth members grow up in single-parent homes. Scouting provides good adult role models.

- It costs approximately $50 to provide a 12-month Scouting experience to a youth member in the Atlanta Area Council.

- For the same cost of maintaining one juvenile in detention for a year in Georgia, we can deliver the Scouting program to 500 youth members.

- Scouting for the Handicapped and In-School Scouting programs are growing and improving each year.

- Exploring offers vocational career-oriented programs for high school age boys and girls.

- Your tax-deductible contribution supports Scouting in your community.

- Over 45,000 youth members were served through Scouting in these counties:

𝔒n my ɦonor
ℑ will do my best...

**ATLANTA AREA COUNCIL
BOY SCOUTS of AMERICA**
100 EDGEWOOD AVE., 4TH FLOOR
ATLANTA, GA 30303
(404) 577-4810

CARROLL	GWINNETT
CHEROKEE	HARALSON
CLAYTON	NEWTON
COBB	PAULDING
DEKALB	PICKENS
DOUGLAS	ROCKDALE
FULTON	

Figure 5.4. Sample campaign brochure (Courtesy of the Atlanta Area Council, Boy Scouts of America.)

most current information in conducting a campaign. It will hurt your campaign if some of last year's information is mistaken for current information, especially when answering questions about service statistics and financial data.

Use of Media in Campaigns

Sooner or later in all volunteer organizations someone will suggest that "if we could just get our story in the paper"—implying that if everyone knew of our work the contributions would automatically flow in. As a general rule, this assumption is not accurate. From time to time newspapers do tell the community of some unusual event, for example, a church burning down, a family burned out, an unfortunate person hurt in an industrial accident. Such stories will result in a genuine outpouring of contributions from the public. Usually, the newspaper will establish a bank account to receive the money and ultimately transfer it to the organization or individual the donors seek to help.

On the other hand, simply getting the needs of your organization before the public in a news story only rarely will generate an unsolicited contribution. However, this does not mean that informing the public is not supportive and helpful to the general campaign.

Announcements of the appointment of campaign leadership are often carried by the news media and provide not only recognition to the individual, but recognition to your organization.

Broadcast Media

Radio and television stations are required to provide a certain amount of air time for public service announcements. When these announcements are well prepared, they are more likely to be aired. Remember, however, that there are hundreds of organizations seeking access to this public service time, and any material you provide to the stations must be well done and must recognize the limitations of this public service. To illustrate, a typical radio spot is 20, 30, or at the most 60 seconds. Therefore, a public service announcement that would take 3 minutes does not stand as good a chance of use as a well-done 20- or 30-second spot sent in by another organization.

Print Media

Newspapers and other print media also tend to recognize their responsibility to the community and will do a good job of providing opportunities for your stories to be in print. However, just as with the broadcast media, newspapers and other print media are being constantly bombarded with news releases and stories from dozens—if not hundreds—of organizations seeking to tell their stories to the public. Do not waste your time and postage on material for the print media if it is not done well, accurately, and in time for the deadlines of the publications.

Make sure that you tell your story through the news media *all year long*. Success stories happen every day, so don't wait until campaign time to share these stories with the press and your public.

Telling Your Story to Prospects

Use a Speakers' Service

Depending on how broad your prospect base is, there are valuable opportunities for direct communication through a speakers' service. Civic and service clubs are abundant in every community, and many are delighted to have guest speakers tell their membership about organization programs. Volunteers, with training and orientation, can do a very effective job of telling your story, particularly if they have had an active involvement in the organization and can attest through personal experience to its success. You may find it helpful to support the speakers' bureau with slides to illustrate the presentation and further ensure that the fundamental message is consistent.

Try a 'Fireside Chat'

Those organizations dealing primarily with a prospect list involving people who utilize the service of the organization or, in the case of youth agencies, the parents of youth members often find it important to conduct special "fireside chat" meetings to discuss the campaign and the program of the organization. These fireside chats can be very effective if they involve key board leadership in helping tell the organization's story. The meetings probably are best done in an informal setting by utilizing, when possible, homes of active organization volunteers.

Year-round Communications

In addition to being important during the campaign time, communication with donors or prospective donors must be a year-round process. Your organization may find that is well worth the time and commitment of both staff and volunteers in such activities.

Such events as an open house, particularly if your organization has a facility where services are delivered, will be helpful. Having prospective donors drop by to see staff dealing with clients is a very effective way to communicate the excitement of the program your organization provides. These events need not be during the course of the campaign if the organization understands the need to have year-round identification and cultivation of prospective donors.

PART 3

Making Effective Presentations

Asking for a gift is the primary objective in organizing volunteers to raise money. Whether you are asking an individual of modest means, a large foundation, a local corporation, or a personal friend, readying yourself to share your story of financial need with a prospect requires preparation, practice, and action. Chapters 6, 7, and 8 will help you prepare to ask!

6
The Corporate Solicitation

Attend almost any gathering of professional fund raisers or key volunteers involved in the management of nonprofit organizations, and you will find that much of the conversation revolves around significant gifts secured from major corporations in the local community. Why? A good football team has 22 first-string players, each playing a critical role in the total success of the team. Each member of the team knows that failure by any one of them can result in a possible loss; yet each inherently knows that the flashy running back, star quarterback, or superaggressive linebacker gets more press coverage than a guard or defensive end. The big play makes news. Steady play that makes big plays possible is just assumed.

Securing adequate financial resources for a nonprofit organization usually involves many prospects giving relatively small annual gifts; yet, like the star player, the large corporate gift tends to bring recognition to the organization, is reported by both the organization and the corporation's public relations staff, and receives accolades at gatherings of people who are involved in financing nonprofit organizations. Securing corporate support can bring you the needed dollars and public recognition. A good annual campaign plan will include corporate solicitation for most organizations.

The general principles of securing a gift from a corporation are not dissimilar to securing a gift from an individual in terms of peer solicitation, case presentation, and prospect selection. However, there are certain procedures that are involved in the corporate decision-making process to support a nonprofit organization that are important for you to understand and utilize in a successful campaign.

The Role of the Gatekeeper

It is fairly common for most corporations—either formally or informally—to have a person who is responsible for monitoring all requests for corporate support by community organizations. Such requests may be for money, equipment, services, or use of facilities. Often this person becomes the access point for these organizations seeking assistance, and as such the person becomes a "gatekeeper," meaning one who is responsible for coordinating requests for support and communicating company policy and response to proposals. The gatekeeper usually wants to respond positively to ensure good community identity. As the number of requests for support increases, seeking community goodwill becomes more difficult as the total dollars requested often exceed the corporation's budget for contributions. The person filling the gatekeeper role often has additional management responsibilities that may limit his or her time for an in-depth investigation of requests for support. Therefore, if you provide helpful information that eases the decision process, you will enhance your probability of a gift. Most often you will find that the gatekeeper, often carrying the title of Vice President for Community Affairs, or Public Relations, or some similar designation, has easy access to the chief executive officer of the corporation.

Five Functions

To understand what the gatekeeper does, it helps to understand what the gatekeeper must do to represent the corporation to the public and help it reach the objectives of the corporation and its key officers. The primary objective is to achieve a positive public image through support of socially responsible programs made possible by community organizations. Seeking to achieve this basic objective—good public relations—defines the following tasks for the gatekeeper.

Monitoring

All requests for assistance are carefully reviewed in line with the goals and objectives of the corporation. These goals and objectives may be very explicit or quite vague depending on the corporation's organizational and operational policies. Has the request come from a highly regarded organization within the community? Will a gift to the organization further enhance the public service image of the corporation? Do any employees of the corporation have a direct interest in the organization? Does the organization represent some cause or issue that might be good for business, if corporation support became known? Is the amount requested in the range of the normal response of the corporation? Does the gatekeeper know anything about the organization or its volunteer leadership? A yes to any of these questions will be a positive influence on the decision to contribute, and a no will decrease the likelihood of a positive response.

Investigation

If the proposal is one that could enhance the public perception of the corporation and its employees and officers, the gatekeeper may contact others within the community seeking information about the organization. This informal gathering of additional information from other sources probably will be done without your knowledge. In most cases, gatekeepers know their counterparts in other corporations. Discussion of your organization with these peers is not unusual. Positive feedback will often lead to a gift, while negative feedback may mean that the request goes no further.

Initiation

Many corporations develop specific areas of interest within a community and corresponding budgets for corporate support. When this is the case, the gatekeeper may seek to communicate with appropriate organizations the company's interests. In some rare instances an unsolicited gift may be made to the nonprofit organization. For example, if the corporation believes it will enhance its public image by an association with the fine arts, the gatekeeper might make informal contacts with representatives, often volunteers, who are actively involved in various organizations in the fine arts. Such discussions could lead to a gift to the local ballet, even if a request has not been received from the group.

Decision Making

If the corporation has a budget for community support, a positive decision will often be made by the gatekeeper if the organization's request for support is in keeping with the practices of the corporation. Most corporations give much of their corporate support out of habit. Did we give this organization a contribution last year? Is the amount requested about what we gave last year? Did we receive any positive feedback from either the organization or the community as a result of this gift? Does what we know about the organization continue to be positive? Often, almost unconsciously, the gatekeeper will review questions such as these, and assuming the answers are all positive, routinely respond with the contribution requested. Likewise, a gatekeeper will enjoy great latitude in denying requests rather routinely, particularly if the corporation has well-defined guidelines on corporate support policies. However, when the gift requested is large, may be of particular interest to a senior officer of the corporation, is from an unknown organization, or appears particularly innovative, the gatekeeper may refer the matter to a "contributions committee."

Evaluation

After a gift is made, the gatekeeper, perhaps intuitively, evaluates how the organization used that gift. Did they apply the gift to the purposes of the proposal? Did the corporation receive any community feedback as a result of their gift, either positive or negative? Do the employees of the corporation feel good about the company's gift? Was appropriate recognition and appreciation for the gift received from the organization? Did the organization report its use of the funds and the results achieved?

These and similar questions are an evaluation of both the organization and the gatekeeper, since one of the major objectives of the gatekeeper on behalf of the organization is to enhance the positive image of the corporation in the community. If you anticipate ongoing support from the corporation, do not forget how important this function is to the gatekeeper and the corporation.

The Contributions Committee

Many fund raisers wonder whether a contributions committee exists as often as it is referred to in rejection letters. While the committee may not be formalized within the corporation structure and may be relatively small in size, one probably does exist. Just as the committee may be informal, the review may be an informal one, done through a memorandum or a brief chat with individual members on the committee. Whatever the process, the gatekeeper often transfers the decision-making function to such a committee.

Committee Composition

In many companies the contributions committee consists of the chief executive officer of the corporation, senior financial officer, and perhaps an officer charged with a public relations function, if that person is not the gatekeeper. Some companies include an employee representative as well.

Large, publicly held corporations may even have a board level committee dealing with contributions and other areas of social responsibility. If there is a board level committee, it is likely to have some of the "outside" directors on the committee. Such committees rely heavily on staff work, and almost always have a corporate employee assigned to staff the committee. The smaller the company, the more likely the CEO will be a member of the contributions committee.

Getting the Proposal to the Committee

Your letter or proposal requesting support, once received by the gatekeeper, may not be forwarded to individual members of the committee. In many cases, a memorandum from the gatekeeper to the committee will state briefly the name of the organization, the amount requested, and most likely a recommendation by the gatekeeper as to an appropriate response. While it is not unusual for the gatekeeper to ask for additional information, it is extremely rare for you to be asked to appear before the contributions committee. The implications of this, of course, would indicate that your request for support must be carefully prepared, clearly communicate the unmet needs of the organization, your capacity to meet these needs, and, most important, what benefits may accrue to the corporation in providing such support. Lack of good information is frequently the reason for denial.

Corporations and their gatekeepers are not looking for a great deal of material, just clear, concise statements that help the company understand what the need is and how a gift from them will be used.

What the Committee Will Want to Know

The questions that will be in the mind of the gatekeeper could include any or all of the following:

Is the proposed project innovative?

Can the results of the project be evaluated?

Will your organization report on the outcomes of the project? When?

Will support of the project enhance our corporation's community image?

Is your organization noncontroversial?

Are any of our employees actively involved with the organization? Who?

Have we made a gift to your organization before? How much did we give you?

Are other corporations in our community being asked to give? How much?

The Annual Contributions Budget

Fund raisers also wonder whether the corporation really does have an annual budget for contributions. Many rejection letters often note that "while the committee was favorably disposed to assist your organization, the budget for the year did not allow a contribution." An annual budget for contributions probably does exist in most corporations, and it probably is formalized in the sense that a total pool for contributions for the year is in writing and is shared with key corporate officers. Therefore, timing is important. Requests for support enhance the probability of success if they tie in to the corporation's budget cycle.

Budget Criteria

Probably the largest single criterion used in establishing a contributions budget is the historical giving record of the corporation in the previous year. In other words, the giving budget of a corporation is normally incremental in nature, rather than the result of a formal budgetary planning process that one might find in budgets developed for a manufacturing or marketing function within the corporation.

Federal law allows corporations to deduct contributions up to 10% of pretax profits, after certain adjustments (Internal Revenue Code Section 170). However, the record clearly indicates that, across the nation, corporate giving has consistently remained under 2 percent of pretax profits.[1] Some corporate budgets may be based on last year's profits, or, in some cases, last quarter's profits, while others may be based on historical patterns. It is highly likely that after the initial creation of a budget for contributions by a corporate support program, succeeding budgets are much more likely to be influenced by historical giving patterns of the corporation rather than by sales or profits. Increasingly, corporations are reporting their support in this area, so it is a good idea to review the most recent corporate annual report for some idea of the type of organizations or causes they support.

Corporate Policy

Some corporations, particularly large, nationally known corporations, tend to develop a formal corporate policy on support for nonprofit organizations. These policies deal with such issues as geographic locations (typically they will give where they have major groups of employees); a "matching gift" program to encourage employee contributions to nonprofit organizations; and, in some instances, program policies such as a commitment to higher education, the arts, and social service agencies. Increasingly, corporations are establishing "matching funds" programs. As these programs grow, it may indicate new ways to approach corporations. Some corporations have specific policies that preclude gifts to nonprofit organizations that are advocacy oriented.

Exceptions to Policy. Even when corporations have established policies that outline to whom they will contribute, in what amounts, and in what areas, it does not mean that an organization that does not meet existing policy criteria will be rejected. As in the case of individual solicitation, if the person who asks is a close friend of the senior officer, a grant may be made regardless of guidelines. For example, a corporation that by policy supports organizations serving areas where its facilities are concentrated, and would normally reject a request for funding that did not meet this criteria, may yet consider making a contribution if the chief executive officer happens to serve on a corporate board with a friend seeking support. The "old boy network" does exist, and it operates very efficiently. While it is rarely ever acknowledged, a primary motivating factor in corporate giving is tied to corporate and personal enhancement through relationships with peers in the community.

Employee Relationships

Another factor that can influence corporate support is the relationship your organization has with employees of the corporation. There are many instances where corporate gatekeepers will respond to individual requests from employees for support of "our Little League team" or a "gift to help our high school debate team go to the state competition," because the corporation's generosity improves its image in the minds of its own employees. News of contributions of this sort travels rapidly through the employee grapevine and helps make each person working there feel that the corporation really cares about the people it employs. The trend to be responsive to employee objectives is increasing. Therefore, it is helpful to utilize your volunteers if practical.

Getting Your Proposal Considered

Prospect Homework

With the gatekeeper, a fixed budget, and corporate policies in place, you must be prepared to do an effective job of prospect research if you hope to have a proposal seriously considered. Public data is readily available in almost all instances about the nature of the corporation, its officers, its size, the location of its facilities, and the like in a variety of published sources as shown in Figure 6.1.

Stay attuned to the leadership patterns in your community through participation in service organizations, daily reading of the local press, and participation in community-wide activities such as the Chamber of Commerce. You must know who the local corporate movers and shakers are.

Exploratory Contact

Probably the two most common initial contacts with a corporation are with the senior corporate official in the community or with the corporate gatekeeper. It is extremely important, if at all possible, to have the initial corporate contact made through a social or business peer and, better yet, a friend of the person to be contacted. If the friendship between the solicitor and the corporate officer is close enough, it may be possible to secure a significant gift with as simple a comment as "John, I have your company's card for the annual United Negro College Fund Drive." The principles of peer solicitation found in individual solicitation work exactly the same for corporate solicitation, between corporate chiefs. Even though the gifts will come from corporate sources, the solicitation is personal—often private—and may depend upon the solicitor's personal friendship.

If your organization's relationship with a corporation is less personal, it's still possible to secure corporate support. A visit by the development director and a key volunteer board member with the corporation's local gatekeeper for an informal chat about the organization's contribution to

Taft Corporate Giving Directory. Comprehensive Profiles of America's Major Corporate Foundations and Charitable Giving Progams. Published annually by the Taft Group, 5130 MacArthur Blvd., N.W., Washington, D.C., 20016.

Corporate 500: The Directory of Corporate Philanthropy. Published annually by Public Management Institute, 358 Brannan St., San Francisco, CA, 94107.

Corporate Foundation Profiles. Published annually by Monitor Publishing Company, Washington, D.C. A listing of the corporate leadership of the Corporate 1000.

National Directory of Corporate Charity. Published annually by the Foundation Center, New York. A listing of 1600 corporate foundations, their leadership and the grants they make.

Sibbal Guide, Corporate Profiles. Published by states. Published by Sibbal Company, Chicago, Ill. Updated regularly.

Dun & Bradstreet, Inc.: through Duns Marketing Service Business Reference Library, publish a number of reference books: Reference Book of Corporate Managements. Biographical profiles of principal officers of more than 12,000 US companies.

Million Dollar Directory. Information on more than 160,000 US businesses including privately held companies, each with a net worth of over $500,000.

America's Corporate Families. A comprehensive listing of over 8,000 US parent companies and their 44,000 domestic divisions and subsidiaries.
ADDRESS: Dun's Marketing Services
        Dun & Bradstreet Corporation
        3 Century Drive
        Parsippany, N.J. 07054

Figure 6.1 Sources of information on corporations.

the community should lead to valuable information about how to approach the corporation, what size gift they might make, and what features of a proposal would be most important to them. Often, the timing of the request is critical, and this information can also be gleaned from an informal chat. For example, the gatekeeper may respond courteously to the visit, but note that this year's budget has been committed and indicate that a request next year would be acceptable and perhaps even invited. In this case, it is important to ask exactly when the corporation's fiscal year begins so that the proposal can be submitted at the most appropriate time. Request a set of guidelines if available and follow them.

Sometimes, exploratory contact with a corporation can be further enhanced if you have a volunteer who is also an employee of the corporation, and is willing to accompany other volunteers on a visit. Such an inside contact must be carefully evaluated to ensure that such an individual feels involved and not used, and at the same time enhances the leverage of your organization with the corporation.

Formal Proposal

After an informal, exploratory contact, most often you will follow-up with a formal proposal or letter outlining the nature of your request and the amount of support requested. If the gatekeeper suggests a letter, it is important to find out to whom the letter should be addressed. Similarly, if a formal proposal is suggested, it is important to inquire about desired contents and types of supporting documentation required.

Your case statement, current budget, a copy of the IRS letter confirming tax deductible status, recent financial statement, and service statistics, are the most frequently requested information. Put your best foot forward and be willing to provide answers to any questions, particularly about your financial operation and delivery of services. Corporations are more willing to consider support of well-managed and effective organizations, than those which appear to be poorly managed or operated. If you have already received support from other corporations active in the community, it may be helpful to indicate who has made a commitment and in what amount. Corporations are strongly guided by "their share."

Personal Presentation

In some rare instances, you may be requested to make a formal presentation to the corporation's chief officer. If this invitation is extended, have one or two members of your board of directors involved in the presentation. Select members who come as close as possible to peer solicitation for this appointment. Make sure that these volunteers are fully briefed about the prospective donor, rehearsed on the presentation delivery, and are prepared to answer questions. Find out how much time you have for the appointment and respect those limits. Although the corporate representative may choose to extend the appointment, you should be prepared to state your case effectively in the time allocated.

'Closing' Your Request

Whether you present your proposal to the gatekeeper or to a corporate officer, as you leave, express your appreciation and leave an attractive folder containing your proposal with the prospect. This small closing technique is important. The written proposal provides tangible evidence of your visit, reinforces your request for corporate support, provides facts that support your performance as an organization, and, most important, requires an answer by the person visited. Most good managers find it impossible to disregard such a request when you leave something tangible. They must either decide on its merits themselves, or refer it to others in the corporation. If they refer it to others for review, it will receive even more attention, thus ensuring a larger corporate audience for the goals and needs of your organization.

Even if you do not ultimately receive a gift from the corporation, you should realize that the visit gave you an opportunity to educate a key community leader, and in many cases made it possible for you to request corporate support in the future.

Recognition

Thanks

Once you secure a gift from a corporate donor, the typical recognition and cultivation procedures that take place for individual donors should be duplicated. A personal letter from your president and perhaps your executive director is the first order of business. Recognition plaques, certificates, or other mementos are often appropriate as well. If you visited the offices of the corporation and saw such on display, it is important that your organization respond in kind.

Publicity

The subject of public recognition is one that should be cleared with the gatekeeper. Some corporations will seek publicity through news releases issued through their public relations department or by your organization. Key leadership in the corporation will often pose for pictures presenting a check. However, some corporations may seek anonymity, fearing a deluge of similar requests for support. When in doubt, ask! If your gift was obtained outside the usual giving policies of the corporation, it's most likely that the corporation will not seek public knowledge of it.

Follow-up

Regardless of the amount of public recognition, it's important to continue contact and involvement with both officers and the company.

Periodic reports on how the corporation's money was spent, a copy of your annual report and audit, invitations to appropriate functions, and recognition of the corporation in your newsletter will improve your chance for ongoing corporate support.

Many corporations appreciate being mentioned in your annual report. If you provide services that directly benefit donor employees, that fact should be made clear to the corporation as well. This also enhances the likelihood of continued support. Despite the modest "Don't thank us" disclaimer you will often hear, it is impossible to show too much appreciation to either individuals or corporations for their support. If such support came through a personal friend, an occasional progress report to the friend is also well worth the effort.

Notes

1. Richard Piperno and Fred Schnaue, *Giving USA: Estimates of Philanthropic Giving in 1985 and the Trends They Show*, American Association of Fund-Raising Counsel, Inc., New York, 1986, p. 33.

7

The Foundation
Solicitation

Foundations Come in All Sizes

As with corporation solicitation, you must understand foundations if
successful proposals are to be made. In 1985, foundations gave over $4
billion to charitable organizations and agencies. There are in excess of
24,000 foundations currently operating in the United States. The
largest, the Ford Foundation, has assets of almost $4 billion. The
Andrew W. Mellon Foundation, Pew Memorial Trust, W. K. Kellogg
Foundation, Robert Wood Johnson Foundation, Rockefeller Foundation, John D. and Catherine T. MacArthur Foundation, and the Lilly
Endowment, Inc., each have in excess of $1 billion in assets. However,
the bulk of the total assets of all foundations does not belong to the large
foundations. Eighty-one percent of the foundations have assets of less
than $1 million, and 60 percent of the foundations have less than
$250,000 in total assets.[1]

As with major corporate donations, large foundation grants often
make the news, while tens of thousands of grants are made annually to
organizations throughout America from relatively small foundations.
The large foundations often make grants on a national or even international basis, and in some cases their areas of interest are restricted to
particular fields or require such comprehensive proposals that most
organizations stand little chance of receiving a grant. However, the
smaller foundations generally lean toward providing grants for local
organizations and sometimes restrict their giving to specific communities
or states.

Why Foundations Exist

All too often people forget why foundations exist. Foundations are created to give money away, and in almost all cases, to nonprofit organizations. Unlike individuals and corporations, who have no legal requirement to give money away each year, foundations must give it away in accordance with strict regulations established by the federal government. They file annual reports with the Internal Revenue Service (IRS 990 AR), and can be and are audited by the IRS to ensure that they meet the legal requirements established by the Congress.

When an organization makes a proposal to a foundation, following the guidelines established by the foundation, you will find the foundation staff and directors cordial and appreciative of your efforts. Your proposal will be carefully reviewed, and, if you meet their criteria, you have a good chance of receiving a gift. When your organization makes a good, timely proposal, you are helping the trustees meet their legal responsibilities as foundation trustees.

Types of Foundations

Rather than deal with a technical or legal definition of a foundation, it is more helpful to explain the types of foundations you may encounter. All foundations can be placed into one of six types. Understanding the differences will help you in developing good proposals and save you time.

1. National/general purpose foundations
2. Special purpose foundations
3. Family foundations
4. Corporate foundations
5. Community foundations
6. Operating foundations

National or General Purpose Foundations

These foundations often fund programs or projects that focus on national or international problems. Some like to fund pilot projects, while others fund projects with high visibility. The size of their grants tends to be large and often payable over a period of years. In some cases, these foundations seek organizations willing to address specific problems of interest to the trustees.

Some foundations may work in cooperation with other funding sources to support a project that needs very large resources over a long time.

These foundations have professional staffs who not only formalize the proposal process, but often provide the board of trustees extensive background investigation of the organization requesting funding totally independent of information provided by the agency. However, remember that they also make small contributions to organizations that propose projects that fit their guidelines. Careful matching of your needs to the interests of these foundations may be worth the time and effort.

Special Purpose Foundations

These foundations come in all sizes, and usually have a specific interest that may have been put in place by the original donor(s) when the foundation was created. They can be good sources for support if your organization has a program that fits in their area of interest. They usually have very explicit guidelines and policies that make clear the type of proposals they are interested in.

Family Foundations

These foundations represent the greatest percentage of the total foundations in existence. Their trustees are often family members or, in some cases, lawyers or bankers who represent the interests of the donor or the family. Getting good information on these foundations is more difficult. Careful research, however, can uncover foundations in this category that may be excellent prospects. They, like special purpose foundations, often have restrictions as to location and interest. Family foundations tend to focus their interests on local needs or specific areas of interests. It is not unusual to find fairly restrictive guidelines for grants. For example, grants may be restricted to specific cities, counties, or states. Some may restrict their gifts to specific types of organizations, such as the arts or education or religious causes. If your organization fits the restrictions of such a foundation, there is an excellent chance your proposal will be funded.

Corporate Foundations

Corporate foundations are created by a company to facilitate its support of worthwhile organizations and causes. Once founded, the corporation is likely to make its annual corporate donation allowed under the tax laws to its foundation. Thus, many corporate donations are actually paid through its foundation. Again, these foundations often have restrictions as to location, interests, and issues they will support. They like to make grants that enhance the corporate image or make their employees happy. Most "matching funds" for employee giving programs come from this type of foundation. They are often interested in a "quid pro quo," since they are interested in increasing the public's feeling of goodwill toward the corporation.

Community Foundations

A growing trend in the foundation sector is the creation of community foundations. Generally, community foundations have two major purposes: (1) to stimulate the establishment of endowments to serve the local community, and (2) to address community needs through the awarding of grants for specific projects.

Community foundations normally receive their funds from many donors rather than a single source. They often play an important role in responding to community needs as perceived by the community's power structure. Their boards of trustees are typically broadly representative of the community and tend to provide support to some service needed in a community through grants to existing organizations.

Six of these community foundations have surpassed $100 million in assets to date. San Francisco, New York, and Cleveland community foundations had assets exceeding $350 million at the close of 1985. Community foundations were the fastest growing category of foundations during the year. Today there are more than 300 community foundations in existence.[2]

Operating Foundations

These foundations are created by nonprofit organizations for the purpose of soliciting and holding contributions from individuals, corporations, and other foundations. Most colleges and universities have such a foundation. Often hospitals, religious groups, and health-related organizations will also have a foundation. They would only rarely make a grant to any group other than the group that created the foundation.

Role of the Executive Director/Secretary

The Foundation Directory will typically provide the name of the executive director or secretary or both as well as a mailing address. If the foundation is fairly large, these people may be full-time employees of the foundation. On the other hand, they may be employees of the bank which holds the assets of the foundation. They may be members of the board of trustees who have agreed to serve as contacts. The executive director or secretary plays a "gatekeeper" function similar to that of the gatekeeper as discussed in Chapter 6.

Four Basic Functions

The executive director/secretary will typically have four basic functions:

1. A monitoring function, involving the screening of requests for support for presentation to the board of trustees, communicating with organizations seeking information or grants, and recommending changes in policies and guidelines.

2. An advisory function, responding to questions by the trustees about the particular organization,

3. An initiation function, seeking out particular organizations that are addressing problems of particular interest to the trustees and

4. A decision function, often serving as a member of the subcommittee of the trustees who make recommendations to the board.

The executive director/secretary usually strongly influences the decision of the trustees in making a grant. His or her interest in the particular project often makes the difference with the trustees. In some instances the executive director may control which proposals the trustees consider.

The Contributions Committee

In most instances, the board of trustees for the foundation becomes the contributions committee. The members of these boards often are family members or corporate officers directly related to the individual(s) or company who created the foundation. Only very large national foundations might have a special contributions committee, and then it would be a subcommittee of the board of trustees.

If a contributions committee exists, it will help to evaluate all proposals to ensure that the proposal and the organization meet the established criteria of the foundation and to recommend that a grant be made or denied.

The Annual Contributions Budget

Purpose of the Budget

It would be unusual for a foundation not to have an annual budget of projected contributions. In many cases foundations have annual budgets projected for several years in advance, because the foundation has made financial commitments to organizations payable over several years. Since the board of trustees is responsible for the management of the assets of the foundation and current law requires that foundations disburse 5 percent of their current asset base each year, the budget for contributions becomes an important management tool.

However, it is unlikely that you will be able to accurately ascertain the foundation's contributions budget for the year. Even if you did, it probably would not provide you much guidance, since the budget probably will be stated in several program categories plus unpaid commitments to other organizations.

Foundation Policy Statements

It is more likely for the foundation to issue a policy statement indicating the types of grants it makes, to whom these grants are restricted, and some idea of the type of projects it is interested in supporting.

For those foundations that do not publish policy statements or annual reports, *The Foundation Directory* will give you some clue as to what type of proposals the foundation is interested in receiving and the range of grants made the previous year. (However, there are thousands of foundations that are not included in *The Foundation Directory*.) Gaining this information prior to solicitation of a foundation is important for the organization in order to enhance its proposal by asking for support for a project of particular interest to the foundation.

It is equally important to save time by not sending a proposal to a foundation that is not interested in the work of your organization. For example, some foundations will not give to state-supported higher education institutions. Others restrict their support to organizations providing services within a specific state. Therefore, it's clear that an organization not meeting these policy requirements is wasting valuable time and resources in making a proposal to such a foundation.

Exceptions to Policy. From time to time, foundations with well-established policies will make grants that are exceptions to policy. These grants happen because of either a shift of interest in the foundation or a special request placed before the trustees by a member of the board who has a special interest in the work of a particular organization or cause. *The Foundation Directory* lists the trustees of the foundation. If you have a board member with a personal contact with a member of the board of trustees of a particular foundation, you might find that this mutual friendship makes it possible to explore the possibility of securing a grant even though the work of your organization does not fall in the foundation's normal areas of interest. Obviously, this tentative exploration should be done with discretion and be carefully developed so that embarrassment for the foundation, or its board of trustees, does not result. In some instances, careful cultivation of the executive director or secretary of the foundation can provide the agency with some clues as to whether a proposal outside the normal giving policies might be welcomed or how a slight modification of the proposal from the agency could fit the interest of the board of trustees.

Matching Gifts

Many company foundations have committed a major portion of their annual contributions to a matching funds policy to encourage employee giving to charitable organizations. You should be aware of the matching funds policies of companies so that your potential donors can maximize their gifts to your organization. It is helpful to determine the place of employment of donors and remind the donor that he or she can double, triple, or even quadruple his or her gift by simply notifying the company that a gift has been made to your organization. A list of company foundations with matching gifts policies can be obtained from CASE— The Council for Advancement and Support of Education.

Getting Your Proposal Considered

Principles of Solicitation

The basic principles for foundation solicitation are essentially the same whether it be a large national foundation with a full-time professional staff, a small local foundation managed by bank officers or local trustees, or a community foundation. Many foundations, particularly large foundations and community foundations, have applications for submitting proposals and often produce annual reports that will provide organizations valuable insight into the giving patterns of the particular foundation.

The Foundation Directory provides the organization valuable information about the foundation, its history, the size of its assets, the range of typical gifts, and the name of the individual to contact.

Do Your Homework. For every foundation grant made, there are probably 50 to 100 proposals that are not. Stories of success and failure are often discussed among fund raisers and key volunteers and may prove or disprove one's particular system for getting a proposal considered. For example, form letters, mailed to every foundation within the state will rarely result in a grant or even a follow-up contact by the foundation. Yet there is always the chance that on a given day a particular executive director of a foundation might respond to such a solicitation. However, keep in mind that foundations support the publication of *The Foundation Directory* in an effort to communicate to organizations the kind of information they need to make carefully considered proposals for funding. It is important to remember that the primary purpose for the creation of the foundation is to make grants to deserving organizations. Foundations need proposals, want proposals, and will usually give careful consideration to all serious proposals presented to them. It is equally important to respect the workload placed on executive directors and secretaries, and to make proposals in a professional manner.

There are a number of publications readily available in most public libraries that will provide an extensive list of foundations. As noted already, one of the most common is called *The Foundation Directory* and is published annually by The Foundation Center, New York, N.Y., to help organizations do their prospect homework. In addition, many foundations produce annual reports and will provide organizations copies of this report if requested. Further, the publishers of *The Foundation Directory* also provide a search service for organizations, and can provide a list of foundations likely to seek proposals in a specific area.

Keep in mind that you normally will fare better approaching foundations within your own state or region, where there is likely to be some prior recognition of the work of your organization, or its leadership. If there are foundations in your community, consider them first, followed by foundations in your state.

Exploratory Contact. If you are dealing with a foundation in your community or state, a call or letter requesting an appointment with the executive director or secretary of the foundation may be worth the effort. This exploratory visit should probably be fairly brief and designed to provide the executive director of the foundation a chance to get to know the organization and its key leadership. It is not the time to present a formal proposal. Discuss the work you are doing and ask for advice about the type of programs or projects the foundation is interested in. It is important to respect the time of the foundation's representative. Be on time and prepared with a concise and effective presentation. Provide plenty of time for reaction by the executive director. Be prepared to answer all questions, or respond in writing to the executive director as quickly as possible.

Because of the expense of travel, I would not recommend an exploratory visit with large, national foundations except in very unusual circumstances. If you have done your homework and believe you have a very strong proposal that fits the foundation's interests very closely, a telephone call seeking advice may do the job, and if not, you will get a feel of the need to make an actual visit.

Submitting Your Proposal.   It is important to time the submission of proposals to the annual budgeting cycle of the foundation. Most foundations will publish their submission deadlines or the dates of meetings of board of trustees. It is important for the agency to recognize and meet these deadlines. In some cases it may improve chances for the organization to be responsive to the fiscal year of the foundation. Proposals offered early in the year may stand a better chance of funding than those proposals received late in the year. If the foundation publishes submission deadlines, follow them!

Proposal Format.   Before making a request for funding from a foundation, understand the format in which the foundation desires to receive proposals. Some foundations accept formal proposals and will actually provide application forms for submission of proposals. Most, however, normally expect a letter requesting the grant plus certain supporting documentation such as the IRS tax exempt certification, a list of the organization's board, and its annual operation budget.

Very few foundations ask for in-person presentations of the grant request, although personal delivery of the proposal by the organization's executive director or key volunteer is often appropriate.

If the foundation accepts supporting material or requests more information, the organization should prepare this material and deliver it in a timely manner. However, it's easy to provide too much information, and the organization should determine from the executive director of the foundation the amount of material he or she wishes to consider for presentation to the board. When in doubt, ask! In almost all cases, the executive director of the foundation will appreciate it.

Cultivation of Foundations Donors

Foundation Recognition

As with individuals and corporations, foundations should be thanked and recognized for their contributions to the work of the organization. Occasionally a foundation may require anonymity. If this is the case, honor carefully this request. Keep your thanks limited to a personal letter to the executive director asking him or her to express your organization's appreciation to the board.

Recognition can be anything from a resolution of thanks adopted by the board and transmitted to the foundation board of trustees to a bronze plaque placed on public display by the organization. When in doubt, discuss this recognition program with the executive director of the foundation.

Even after the formal thanks is expressed, it is a good idea for the agency to stay in contact with the executive director of the foundation on a regular basis, looking for opportunities for additional recognition or thanks throughout the year.

Publicity.   News releases announcing foundation gifts can bring recognition to your organization and the foundation. It is important to clear the release of this information with the executive director in advance. Since foundations are created to make grants, I have found that most foundations do not object to news releases, but want the information about the foundation and the grant it has made to be accurate.

The Close-out Report

Even if the foundation does not require them, it is good to provide systematic reports on the progress of the organization toward its objectives. Once the grant funds have been spent, a final report to the foundation thanking them for the grant and providing a report on the results achieved may help with future proposals. It is surprising how many organizations fail to do this rather simple task. Do not be lulled into complacency because the grant is from a foundation. Keep in mind that individual people make the decisions about the foundation's grants, and they like to feel good about your successes, which they helped to bring about.

Notes

1. Richard Piperno and Fred Schnaue, *Giving USA: Estimates of Philanthropic Giving in 1985 and the Trends They Show,* American Association of Fund Raising Counsel, Inc., New York, 1986, p. 26.

2. Ibid., pp. 29–30.

8

Making a Personal Solicitation

Many people find it difficult, if not impossible, to ask another person for a contribution. The discomfort is so strong that they will find a hundred excuses not to get involved in a campaign. If they find themselves committed to help in a campaign, they will be the procrastinators that cause the campaign to bog down and fail to meet its goal.

Almost everyone that agrees to help in the campaign needs training in making a solicitation, constant encouragement, and moral support. Some will not make contacts, or the contacts will be "half-hearted" or apologetic, and thus not very effective. To help your solicitors overcome discomfort and procrastination, teaching them how to make a call must be a part of the campaign schedule. To reduce the number of solicitors that fail to make calls or make ineffective calls, insist that solicitors participate in adequate training and preparation for making calls. To keep your campaign on schedule, hold regular report meetings and personal follow-up with your workers, encouraging them to finish their personal contacts.

Training Needed

Training individuals to become effective solicitors can be incorporated into the meetings that are a part of the campaign process discussed in Chapter 4. Since the actual solicitation is the point at which individuals decide to contribute, training for more effective presentations becomes central to success in your campaign. Many volunteers will be reluctant to spend much time in "training," offering the excuse that they have done it before or "they helped with the Heart Fund last year." They will ask for their cards and promise to make the calls. While some of your volunteers have been active with your organization and have successfully made solicitation contacts in the past, most have not, and they need training and encouragement throughout the campaign. Use people that truly need no additional training in volunteer leadership positions in your current campaign. They become "trainers" for other volunteers because they know how to do it well.

It is helpful to call your training sessions "orientations" or "kickoff meetings" to reduce the natural reluctance of many to participate in training. No matter what you call it, make sure that training is done at some gathering of your campaign volunteers.

The Solicitation Process

Making an effective solicitation call is divided into three phases: preparation, practice, and presentation. In many ways, asking someone to make a financial contribution to your organization is not much different from asking someone to buy your house, your car, or your company's product. People who have successful experience in selling often become very good at soliciting others for financial contributions. After all, when you think about it, a solicitor is "selling" the prospect on the values of the organization's work and asks the individual to support the work of the organization by making a contribution.

Preparation

Know Your Product. The next time you make a major purchase, observe the behavior of the salesperson who helps you. Good salespeople know their products. They know what it will do, how it's made, its features, its benefits, its specifications. They can answer your questions. They do it with authority that comes from not only knowing the product or service, but believing that it has value to you, the customer. Good salespeople practice what they preach. Automobile salespeople drive the automobiles they sell. Shoe salespeople wear the shoes they sell. It is more than just the employee discount, it is belief that comes from product knowledge.

Professional salespeople often participate in sales meetings to learn more about their products or to see and experience new products.

Likewise, it is important for your solicitors to know the services of your organization well. What do you do? How well do you do it? What are the benefits to your clients, contributors, and the community at large? How does your organization function? Who is on the board of directors? Where does your financial support come from? How do you spend your budget each year? These questions illustrate the basic thrust of helping volunteers prepare for presenting your case to potential contributors.

How much should they know? A difficult question. Volunteer time is limited, and you can't keep training solicitors forever because the campaign must stay on schedule. Be realistic and develop the basic information about the work of your organization that helps the solicitor know the story he or she will tell. A good case statement is a start. Usually a brochure, the case statement contains budget information, service statistics, and success stories describing human outcomes. Pictures show the work of the organization in action. Hopefully, your solicitor will have had some previous involvement with your organization so some knowledge will be from personal experience. As good salespeople understand, knowing how to get answers to questions that can't be answered on the spot is also part of the training. Who does the solicitor call if he or she needs additional information?

Research Your Prospect. The preparation phase also includes some analysis by the solicitor of the prospects he or she is to call on. Are any of the prospects personal friends or business associates? Do they share common work experiences? Is it best to see the individual at his or her place of work, or at home? Does the prospect have any previous record of supporting your organization? Are any of the prospects active in common community activities I participate in?

The more the solicitor knows about the prospect, the greater the chance of success in making a request for financial support. While information about your organization is readily available and is in printed material, the source of information on prospects will probably be very limited within the official records of your organization, but may be available through personal experiences or mutual friends of the solicitor.

Practice

Practice makes perfect is an old saying that adults often use with their children, but are reluctant to apply to themselves. Good solicitors are developed through successful experience. The initial solicitation experience is greatly enhanced with practice before the presentation.

Practice with Others. There are many ways to practice during the training phase of the campaign. Slide shows, video tapes, or demonstrations can be used effectively. Watching someone else make a presentation helps the learner apply the principles to himself or herself. Teaming with another solicitor to "role play" the actual presentation is a very strong reinforcement and should be encouraged. If you have the resources to do it, using video to record the role-play experience and play it back for critique will add more reality to your training. This can make some volunteers very uncomfortable, so make sure you have a person participate who really does volunteer to try this experience.

Visualize Success. Mental practice is helpful and will increase the possibility of success when the real experience is played out. Many leaders in sports, politics, art, and business have developed the ability to mentally "see" themselves going through an experience successfully. A baseball player might mentally "see" the pitch coming and watch himself connect with the ball and follow it as it goes out of the park for a homerun. He even continues to "see" himself circling the bases and being greeted by members of his team at home plate. Successful salespersons accomplish the same thing by picturing themselves making their presentation to the client, answering questions, and getting the signed contract.

Regardless of the method, practice does make perfect, or, at the least, increases both the likelihood of the solicitor making the first call and receiving a positive response.

With volunteers, it also helps to make the practice fun. Get everyone involved. Give a prize to the best "role player." Congratulate all who give it a try. Let a few successful solicitors tell briefly of their initial experiences. However, be careful with letting volunteers tell their "war stories" as they often overdo it and make it sound tougher than it was in reality. Discuss this concern with anyone making such a presentation in advance.

Make the Easiest Call First. Some people, even with preparation and practice, will still be reluctant to make the first call. When someone is this concerned, one final suggestion may help. Suggest that the first request for support be to someone they know. Tell the solicitor to tell the person that this is his or her first try at raising money for your organization and that he or she is scared to death. In almost every case, a friend wants the solicitor to feel comfortable and will help the person through the presentation by asking questions if necessary. An honest statement of fear and an implied request for help will usually lead to encouragement and a donation. Americans love to help each other, even when it involves making a contribution.

Presentation

A solicitation does not happen until someone asks a prospect for a gift. Public service advertisements, good campaign material, excellent training, enthusiastic campaign leadership, and outstanding service statistics mean little until an individual is asked by another to make a contribution.

Committed volunteers, using good prospects that have been carefully identified and evaluated, will get results in the great majority of all solicitations. Americans are a generous people, trained by their religious and cultural heritage to be responsive to those in need. While not every prospect will give when asked, 9 out of 10 people do make contributions each year. The primary reason they make contributions is because someone asks them. If they know the person asking, almost 8 out of 10 will make a gift.[1]

Be aware that generally most cards of prospects returned by solicitors with no response were not asked. In some cases you can reassign these cards to other solicitors. Despite the training you provide, some will decide on their own that the prospect can't make a gift. Remind your solicitors often to let the prospect make up his or her own mind about a contribution. The solicitor's job is to ask for the gift on behalf of your organization.

Call for an Appointment.   Society has changed a great deal in the past several decades, and we no longer live next door to our friends and associates. Many households have both the husband and wife employed. Many prospects are living alone. While some contacts may be accomplished by the solicitor by "dropping in," today, almost everyone will be more successful by calling for an appointment. If the prospect must know the nature of the visit, suggest that the solicitor say that he or she has a favor to ask, and would prefer to do it personally. If your solicitor selected the prospect cards he or she is to call on, calling for an appointment isn't difficult. Also, remember that calling for an appointment is the first step in the presentation process, and it will help your solicitor finish the process.

Once the appointment is set and the solicitor is with the prospect, the actual presentation is fairly simple. Solicitors will be better off if they develop a style they are comfortable with.

Seek Areas of Common Interests. Start the visit like any conversation that is normal in social contacts. Briefly review the friendship if appropriate. If possible, mention mutual friends that may be involved in the work of the organization. Thank the person for his or her time to discuss an important matter of concern. Start with a brief personal history of experience with the organization. Tell the prospect that you are working on a campaign to raise money to support the work of your organization. Ask the prospect if he or she is familiar with your organization.

Listen for Interests and Values. In most cases, the prospect will give you clear signals of his or her community interests, good experiences with your organization, or share a warm memory from the past that relates to the type of organization you are helping. If you detect little evidence of community involvement or support, it is helpful to reinforce the good experiences you have had from your involvement with the organization: friends you have made, people that have overcome a problem, or recognition it has brought you.

Identify Common Ground. Give the case statement to the prospect, telling him or her how the organization accomplishes objectives that you both feel are important. Explain that you personally chose the prospect's name to call on because you believe that the work of the organization will be of interest to the prospect. Briefly state the objectives of the campaign in terms of the services to be provided for the clientele of your organization. Ask a series of questions that lead the prospect to respond positively, such as "Wouldn't it be good for the neighborhood children to have a safe playground nearby?" or "Don't you agree with me that the crisis hotline is good for our community?" Ask if the prospect has any questions.

Present the Asking Price. Indicate that you have already made a personal financial commitment to the campaign, and ask the prospect to consider joining you as a supporter. You are establishing the "price" of contributing. Suggesting a gift size is helpful to the prospect. He or she then knows what is expected in the transaction. Prospect cards have been rated by the campaign organization before they were selected, and you should know what the requested amount is in advance.

A comfortable way to establish the giving level is a softer approach such as; "I am a Century Club member in our Y. Century Club Members contribute $100 a year."

Discuss Giving Methods.   Remind the prospect that you are seeking a pledge that can be paid monthly, quarterly, or semiannually. In some cases, the gift can be made through use of a bank credit card or a bank draft system.

Ask for the Gift.   By this time in your presentation, you have shared mutual concerns, the prospect is aware of your personal involvement *and* financial commitment, and you have explained how a gift might be made. Hopefully, the prospect has some idea of the size gift you are expecting.

It is all too easy to forget to ask for the gift at this point. Don't, or you will fall short of success. If the gift would make the contributor a member in any sense of the word, you might say, "On behalf of the board, I want to invite you to join our Century Club with your gift of $100." If there is no sense of membership, you might say, "I would like you to consider enrolling with us with a gift of $100."

At this point, one of five responses is likely:

1. OK or Sure, I'll help you. If you get this response, thank the prospect and get the pledge card signed.

2. No, I can't help you. Thank the person for listening and ask if you have left something out in your presentation.

3. No, not right now. Explain the pledge system and suggest a pledge that can be paid later.

4. I would like to think about it, or I need to discuss this with my spouse. Offer to return in a day or two.

5. The prospect asks a question. Since most people dislike saying "no" to a friend, they often start with a question or two. Listen carefully to the question. Hopefully you will be able to tell the difference between a real interest in more information and a question that is really an objection. After answering each question to the best of your ability, give the prospect a reason he or she should make a gift. For example, you might say, "Your gift of $100 would make it possible for two youngsters to spend a week in camp with us this summer." Ask the prospect to join with you again. If you cannot answer the question, tell the prospect you will get the answer and come back for another visit.

Set Up a Follow-up Visit.   The prospect may insist, "I'll have to think it over." The best response is to accept the need for additional time and suggest returning the following day. Acceptance of a return visit is a good sign, while a reluctance to have you return is a bad sign. If the prospect wants to say no but does not want to say it to your face, he or she will suggest that the answer will be mailed to you or your organization. Don't leave the pledge card! Tell the prospect that you are responsible for the card and would feel better if you return with the card at a convenient time. The pledge card is the main control in keeping accurate records, and you complicate matters for your organization and other volunteers when you leave it. If the card is not returned in a reasonable time, another follow-up is necessary to account for the card.

If you still have a no after returning, thank the prospect for his or her time, leave the campaign literature with him or her, and leave. You've done all you could.

Send a Thank-you Note.   Even though your organization will be sending a formal acknowledgment, a personal note of thanks is even better. You and your organization have gained a new friend, and his or her involvement will be enhanced by your note. It's even good to thank the "no" responses, since they did share their time with you and they may become supporters in the future.

Notes

1. Virginia Ann Hodgkinson and Murray S. Weitzman, *The Charitable Behavior of Americans: Findings from a National Survey*, Independent Sector, Washington, D.C., 1985, p. 22.

PART 4

Special Fund-raising Techniques

There is more than one way to raise money! On some occasions, you may need major funding for capital improvements. Using mail to expand your donor base may be necessary. Conducting special events is a way to raise money and expose your programs to more people. Helping potential contributors make contributions that will extend their support to you beyond their lives may help you establish endowments that will become a major source of annual operating support. This section will review many of these techniques in detail and show you how to enhance your fund-raising efforts.

9

Raising Money through Special Events

When volunteers and professional fund raisers get together to discuss how to raise this year's budget or find the funds necessary to start a special project, sooner or later someone will suggest staging a special event to raise the funds needed. Often someone will describe a recent dinner he or she attended that honored a distinguished community leader. Tickets were sold to corporations, organizations, and individuals at a price that clearly exceeded the price of the banquet and related expenses.

To many, this sounds like a great idea! It seems to solve several problems. It helps educate a large group of people about the work of the organization. It gains favorable publicity. It seems easier than recruiting and training the campaign volunteers needed to conduct a traditional campaign. And, in the minds of many volunteers, it seems easier to sell tickets than to ask for a contribution. Some will even suggest that you will attract new people because a lot of people will want to join in honoring the distinguished citizen.

Dinners, receptions, special performances, celebrity golf tournaments, and other activities *may* be a good source of income if conducted effectively. They are very time consuming. If poorly promoted, they end up costing more to stage than the income produced. In some cases, the activity may call on promotional skills not readily available in the organization. Therefore, consider these simple principles before starting a fund-raising activity.

Remember These Principles

Income Must Exceed Expenses

The most important principle seems obvious, but is difficult to accomplish. Income must exceed expenses. If it doesn't, you will fail to accomplish your basic objective of raising money *and* you will compound your problem by spending money you have already raised for other purposes. Since most organizations have fund-raising costs ranging from about 5 percent to 15 percent when they conduct the traditional annual campaigns discussed in Chapter 4, it is easy to get so excited about a "new idea" that you fail to fully understand the total costs of staging an activity. The costs of conducting the event can easily exceed 50 percent of gross revenue. Even if you are successful in getting some services or products donated, many things must be purchased. For example, the activity may require the rental of a hotel banquet room, a golf course, or an exhibition facility or similar location. If a dinner is the format, the meal and service will cost money. The higher the ticket cost, the better the quality of the meal expected by the guests. Add to that the cost of printing tickets, programs, decorations, perhaps travel and housing expenses for special participants, and maybe even advertising, and the costs will add up quickly.

Calculate Your Breakeven Point

Before you begin the project, know how many people—at what price—must attend to cover your costs. Let's look at an example. A dinner at a local quality hotel will be held with an expected attendance of 300. You believe you can sell tickets for $100 per person. As seen in Figure 9.1, your fixed costs (those costs you must pay regardless of how many attend) are $6000, and your variable costs (meal and reception price per person) are $40 per person. Therefore, you must sell 100 tickets to "break even." Figure 9.2 illustrates the effect of selling only 175 tickets. Your income drops to $17,500, leaving you a net of $4500!

In addition to selling tickets to a special dinner, you can improve the bottom line by selling sponsorships. For example, a corporation may pay the cost of the guest speaker's fee, travel, and accommodations. Your dinner program may include "ads" sold to corporations, professional groups, or individuals. Companies or individuals may help with some of the costs by "gifts-in-kind" donations, providing transportation for out-of-town guests, hotel accommodations, printing of the dinner tickets and program, entertainment, and facilities costs. Any "sponsorship" of these costs, which are reflected in your fixed costs noted on the budget,

---

Proposed Dinner Budget

Estimated income:

300 people at $100 each	$30,000

Estimated expenses:

Fixed costs:

Printing, postage, audiovisual rental, awards, music, promotion, decorations and nonpaid meals	6,000

Variable costs:

300 Reception at $10 per person	3,000
300 Dinners at $30 per person	9,000
Total costs:	$18,000
Net revenue:	$12,000

Breakeven Analysis:

Total fixed costs	=	$6,000
Variable cost per person	=	$40
Selling price per ticket	=	$100
Net ticket price per person	=	$60
(Price: cost of dinner)		

$$\frac{\text{Total fixed costs}}{\text{Net ticket price per person}} = \text{Breakeven Point}$$

$$\frac{\text{TFC } \$6,000}{\text{NTP } \$60} = \text{BEP } 100$$

Figure 9.1. Proposed dinner budget

reduces the amount of your fixed costs and increases your net income. While many organizations have raised and continue to raise a lot of money by conducting such activities, many others have lost money or have netted very little. In the latter case, the public may believe that the event was a tremendous success even though the dollars available for the basic purposes of the organization have grown very little.

175 at $100		$ 17,500
Less:		
Fixed costs	$6,000	
Variable costs 175 at $40	$7,000	
	$13,000	−13,000
Net revenue:		$ 4,500

Figure 9.2. Effect of reduced ticket sales

Impact on Operating Funds

If the purpose of using an activity is to raise operating funds for the use of the organization during the current year, you must be prepared to deal with success. If your organization stages a successful celebrity golf tournament and nets $30,000 for operations, how will you raise $30,000 next year? Can you conduct another celebrity golf tournament next year? Will it be as successful financially? Do you want to do it every year? Are other organizations staging similar activities, and are they approaching the same prospects for participation? If the activity cannot be repeated each year with similar success, your organization must be prepared to increase the annual campaign goal by $30,000. Given your current success level, can you add 300 contributors at $100 next year?

Impact on the Annual Campaign

A third principle to consider is what effect the activity will have on your current contributor base. If your current contributors are the people you expect to support the activity by attending and buying tickets, you may find that the prospect feels that he or she has provided your organization the support it deserves for the year. It may be difficult to get your regular supporters to understand that the annual support they have been giving continues to be needed.

Effect of "Community Competition"

In many larger metropolitan communities, there may be one additional principle to remember. Activities such as those already discussed generate a lot of publicity in the community. This publicity stimulates other organizations seeking financial support to try the ideas as well. Since corporations and professional organizations are often the primary prospects for ticket sales, there may be some resistance within the community to buying another table for yet another good cause. This could have a negative effect on your program. If your community already has a great number of fund-raising activities, be very realistic in assessing your potential participation and your ability to have your event be perceived as an event that deserves attendance. Some communities have so many of these "charity affairs" that some organizations have hit upon a novel idea of staging a "nondinner," asking prospects to buy tickets for a dinner. Then the invitation suggests that no one needs "another dinner out" and says stay home and enjoy an evening of relaxation. The initial success of such efforts proves again that if trained volunteers ask for support from their peers, the response will be forthcoming in many cases. It also proves that organizations are always on the look-out for new ways to ask for financial support.

Types of Special Events to Raise Money

Every month, some organization stages a new activity seeking to raise money. Almost all of these activities fall into one of the following categories.

Special Meals

While the majority are still dinner parties, more and more lunches and even breakfasts are being used to accomplish the same objectives. The basic format is a special invitation to a meal from a chairperson with wide name recognition. Tickets are sold at a cost that exceeds the cost of staging the event. Purchase of the ticket may be tax deductible as a contribution. Often the meal will have a featured speaker to attract a larger audience or honors some community leader for his or her contributions to the community or the sponsoring organization. The assumption is that many of the friends of the honoree will want to share in this special occasion, leading to increased ticket sales to prospects not normally reached by the organization.

For example, the board chairperson at a large corporation may be honored for both personal and corporate service to the community. The corporation will send many officers and employees to attend the dinner. Often tables of 6 to 10 seats are marketed to corporations for this purpose. In most cases, the person being honored is asked for a list of friends and business associates for promotion purposes. The activity will have a large dinner committee, each member of which will be expected to help with ticket sales.

Receptions

Similar to meals, receptions, cocktail parties, openhouses, and teas are used as fund-raising events. The elements of a successful dinner can be equally successful without the expense of a meal. Programs tend to be shorter, often with a presentation ceremony for an honoree. As with dinners, people are invited to buy tickets to attend. In some communities there are people who have large homes that most of the potential prospects have never had occasion to visit. Having a person hold the event in such a home attracts some people who would not respond to other invitations. Also, organizations have found it easier to gather social peers in homes rather than public facilities and thereby increase attendance with some groups.

Sporting Events

Golf tournaments, football games, bowling matches, road races, and tennis tournaments, are examples of sporting events used to raise money for not-for-profit groups. For example, a golf course is rented for a day. Foursomes are sold at $125 per player. Volunteers in the organization are organized to sell foursomes to their friends or corporations. Often the organization will secure donated prizes from suppliers of golfing merchandise to award to winners of the tournament. The event starts with light refreshments or lunch and then a "shotgun" start. Each foursome starts on a different hole on the course at the sound of a shotgun blast. This way, 18 groups can start and finish at about the same time. After each group has completed 18 holes, their scorecards are tallied by a team of volunteers. Usually the tournament uses a handicapping system that makes the tournament competitive regardless of golfing skills. A ceremony follows with the awarding of prizes. In some cases local celebrities such as prominent football players or coaches, television personalities, political figures, and perhaps a professional golfer or two, agree to play. Locally recognized celebrities may help enroll the rest of their foursome. Otherwise, individuals are assigned to a foursome led by a celebrity. With handicapping, the celebrities do not have to be good golfers, just good sports.

Some golf tournaments on the PGA tour are "charity events," meaning that the proceeds, after prize money and expenses, go to a recognized charity. The staging of these events is extremely complex and beyond the scope of this book and the capacity of most organizations. While they are fund-raising activities, securing a nationally recognized event is rarely possible. Remember that the sporting event is just a way to solicit individuals or groups to buy tickets to an event that will realize more income than expenses. Such events are popular because of the socialization of peers that happens in such an activity and the willingness of some volunteers to make this type of solicitation, whereas they may not be willing to make the type of solicitation calls required in an annual fund-raising campaign.

Auctions

Products and services such as television sets, boats, residential building lots, restaurant meals, tickets to sporting events, and weekend accommodations at resort hotels are some of the basic ingredients of this type of activity. Volunteers seek donations of products and services from local corporations and businesses. The organization then has an event where people attend and bid on items just as they would at a commercial auction. The successful bidder secures the item and writes the check to the organization.

Variations include staging the auction in conjunction with a dinner; silent auctions where prospects can view the items and submit a written bid, with the highest bidder getting the item; and using television or radio to reach a large public audience, who phone in bids and pick up the items when they deliver a check for the bid amount to the organization.

Exhibitions and Performances

Art shows, orchestra concerts, scout shows, and pet shows are examples of this type of fund-raising activity. Most often, tickets are sold. The event is widely publicized and is open to the public. Tickets can be nominally priced and marketed to a broad audience, or can be relatively expensive and marketed similar to a special dinner program. Where seating is limited, as with a benefit performance of an orchestra, higher priced tickets would be sold.

Some variations include having another organization stage the event and agree to provide a certain percentage of sales to your group. This arrangement is usually called a benefit, and may involve your organization in active promotion and sale of tickets. Some care should be taken in such an arrangement. Some groups may seek to use the positive image of the organization to help increase attendance at a commercial event. Not-for-profit organizations should be very careful not to identify themselves with activities that may alter the positive perception the public has of the organization.

"Thons"

This phenomenon continues successfully in some communities. Telethons, radiothons, bikeathons, runathons, swimathons, and walkathons illustrate this activity. Individuals are asked to contribute to an organization during a broadcast on television or radio. Since many organizations did not have the resources to secure broadcast time, a new generation of thons developed where individuals participate in a walk, run, or ride and seek sponsors for each mile the individual completes. While some of the more famous of these type activities have been successful in the past, many have proved to be very costly to stage in terms of money and volunteer time. Public exposure of the program of the organization often appears to make the effort and expense worth it, but careful analysis should be done each time to make sure the benefits exceed the costs.

Games of Chance

In some parts of the country, a major social event of the week is the Bingo game. Often staged by a nonprofit organization or staged by a promoter who gives some part of the net proceeds to a charity group, many people enjoy participating in these activities. Since there are usually prizes for the winners, the people participating may or may not be aware of the use of the proceeds.

Raffles are also popular. Volunteers in organizations sell "chances," usually at a nominal fee, and a winner is drawn at some occasion. Prizes may be appliances such as television sets, automobiles, or vacations at a resort area. In many cases, the actual prizes may be donated by merchants as a way to seek a good public image within the community. Even when the prize must be purchased, the organization can raise a good amount of money if enough chances are sold. The costs of running raffles are small if prizes are donated.

However, use of games of chance may be illegal in your state or governmental jurisdiction. State and local laws differ considerably across the nation. It may be a violation of state gambling laws. The activity may take a special license or bonding. If your organization is considering this type of activity, seek legal advice before you start.

Organizing to Conduct
Special Events

Once a decision is made to consider using an activity as a source of income, the organization should carefully organize volunteers to perform functions much as it does in an annual campaign. Creation of a steering committee for the event is a good way to start. Chaired by an effective leader, such a committee will follow most of the functions outlined in Chapter 4 for conducting an annual fund-raising campaign. Sufficient lead time needs to be established so that volunteers can be recruited, trained, and organized into an effective group. Since many elements of an activity depend on schedules of individuals and facilities, some organizations find it necessary to book fund-raising activities years in advance. The bigger the project, the longer the lead time.

In addition to a general chairperson and vice chairperson, the steering committee will probably need chairpersons for program, facilities, finance and ticket sales, and promotion and publicity. Depending on the type of activity and the people the organization expects to reach as purchasers of tickets or contributors, there may need to be a prospects chairperson as well. For example, a golf tournament that succeeds must have a well-developed prospect list, with names assigned to carefully selected "salespersons." On the other hand, a telethon seeks a broad public audience, and in this case the publicity committee will be of major importance.

Regardless of the activity, at some point, someone must ask individuals, corporations, or organizations for contributions, gifts of merchandise, or purchase of a ticket. This may be done personally among peers, it may be done through the mail with an invitation, or it may be done over the public airwaves. As with annual campaigns that succeed, the bigger the asking price, the greater the need for personal solicitation and follow-up with assigned prospects.

Tax Deductibility of Activity Contributions

Current Internal Revenue Service codes and regulations allow individuals and corporations to deduct contributions to qualified charities. The gift must be to a religious organization or an organization that has received approval from the IRS as a 501-(c)-3 organization. However, in those situations where the contributor receives some benefit from the gift, only the amount that exceeds the normal price of the benefit received is deductible. This means for example that if a person purchases a ticket for $100 for a special dinner seeking to raise money, only the amount of the ticket that exceeds the dinner's fair market value is deductible. Organizations using activities to raise money should be prepared to advise contributors on the amount of the gift/ticket that is probably tax deductible. It is important to note there are many positive reasons for staging fund-raising activities other than the income received. Enhanced public recognition for the organization, identifying new prospects for solicitation in future campaigns, attracting new members or clients, favorable news coverage, providing a service to the community, and recognizing community leadership are some examples.

Also keep in mind that staging activities helps train volunteers in program delivery and fund raising. Any of these benefits may well be worth the relatively small net income from activities.

One Final Caution

Staging a successful event to raise money can take a great deal of volunteer and staff time. It is easy to forget how much time is involved; if the net payoff to the organization does not justify the time required to succeed, such an approach to fund raising should be passed up for better results with volunteers and staff. Make sure you analyze the cost/benefit ratio of time and the positive benefits of public recognition that follow successful activities. Figure 9.3 is a checklist for planning and conducting a special event to raise money. Depending on the size and nature of your event, you can modify the check sheet to suit your purposes. If, for example, you have a golf tournament, your facilities group would be securing a golf course instead of a banquet hall. If you are not having a guest speaker, delete that part of the check sheet. Events

---

Special Event Check Sheet

Steering committee:
- Recruit a steering committee chairperson.
- Recruit chairpersons for program, finance, and ticket sales and promotion/ publicity.
- Hold regular report meeting prior to event.
- Conduct a postevent evaluation with recommendations for future events.

Program:
- Establish event date and time.
- Speaker identified, confirmed.
- Accommodations for speaker.
- Transportation for speaker.
- Biographical information for publicity.
- Master of ceremonies secured.
- Dinner music/entertainment.
- Honoree identified and secured.
- Biographical information for publicity.

Figure 9.3. Special events check sheet

- Accommodations for honoree.
- Special guests identified and invited.
- Invocation.
- Opening ceremony.
- Introducer for guest speaker.
- Presenter for honoree.
- Recognition piece for honoree.

Facilities:
- Banquet hall located and reserved.
- Contract for banquet hall signed.
- Dinner menu selected.
- Table layout agreed to with hotel.
- Head table decorations.
- Individual table decorations.
- Table number stands.
- Table assignments.
- Head table assignments.
- Reception room layout and decorations.
- Printed programs at each place.
- Podium with light.
- Special lighting for program.
- Special stages needed.
- Sound system ordered and tested.
- Audiovisuals if needed.
- Audiovisuals installed and tested.
- Information/ticket tables at entrance.
- Head table placecards in place.
- Awards in place for presentation.
- Flashlights.
- Drivers for VIPs.
- Set-up and take-down supervision.
- Develop master script.

(Continued)

Figure 9.3. *(Continued)*

Develop subscripts for:
  Introduction of speaker
  Introduction for master of ceremonies
  Introductions of honoree
  Other people on the program
• Brief each program participant on script.

Finance and ticket sales:

• Develop a master budget for the event.

• Develop ticket price and breakeven point.

• Recruit ticket sales teams.

• Develop prospect lists for table sales and individual sales.

• Develop invitation and mail.

• Set up personal solicitation teams for table sales.

• Secure sponsors for special projects, including:
  Transportation
  Accommodations
  Program ads
  Speaker's fees
• Distribution of tickets.

• Assignment of tables.

• Audit income/expense statements and report to board.

Promotion and publicity:

• Design and print invitation.

• Design and print tickets.

• Design and print dinner program.

• Secure radio/TV coverage of dinner.

• Predinner radio/TV spots.

• News releases on speaker, honoree, etc.

• Photographer at dinner.

• Postdinner news releases with pictures.

• Host press table at dinner.

• Develop press kit for press.

• Set up and coordinate radio/TV interviews.

---

such as walkathons would also have to include certain arrangements with governmental authorities related to routes, street closing, etc. As you develop a special event, use the check sheet as a memory jogger and add those items that will ensure that you do not forget any detail that will cause problems with your event.

10

Raising Money through Direct Mail

Many organizations use direct mail as a part of their overall strategy to solicit annual operating funds. They use it not as a replacement for the traditional annual campaign of personal solicitation, but as a way of reaching prospects they cannot reach personally or to increase their donor base by asking new prospects to consider support of their organization with the idea that these donors become part of future annual campaigns. Using the mail can be a productive part of any organization's annual fund-raising plan.

Some organizations use direct mail to raise a major portion of their annual operating budgets. If your organization has a limited natural constituency that identifies with your organization and few volunteers that support your work, direct mail may be a way to develop significant support over time.

If you have a good base of volunteers, using the mail to solicit funds should be only a part of an annual plan to secure operating funds for the organization. The fundamental technique of asking for operating funds through personal solicitation of carefully selected prospects, will give you the base of support you need for strength. As noted in Chapter 3, people give to people when they are asked. The larger the gift requested, the greater the need for the personal solicitation.

Effective Uses of Direct Mail

Renewing Gifts in the Annual Campaign

If your current donor base is so large that you find it all but impossible to secure enough solicitors for personal contacts, you may well want to glean from your current donors those contributors that have been giving at modest levels and you have reason to believe will continue at modest levels. Prospects you don't expect to contact personally or by phone are asked for a gift by direct mail.

As a Follow-up

You may use mail as a follow-up at the end of your annual campaign to ask for a gift from those prospects that were included in your annual campaign for personal contact but were not called on. It is not unusual to have cards of previous donors returned by solicitors at the end of the campaign that were not contacted. Since many of these people are previous givers, it is important to ask them to continue their support.

Increase Your Donor Base

You may make mail contacts part of your annual campaign to increase your donor base for future campaigns. Use the techniques outlined in Chapter 4 on how to secure names of prospects. Each name will have been recommended by a volunteer. If you get more names than you can effectively organize to call on, these names can be asked to give through direct mail.

If you cannot get enough new names from volunteers, direct mail is a way you can tell your story and your needs to a large number of people. Those who respond with a gift can be added to your donor base and included in the appropriate campaign plan for future solicitations.

Make Direct Mail a Part of Your Total Plan

Regardless of the reason you decide to use mail, it is best to make the decision as a part of your overall campaign strategy, rather than as an after-thought when your campaign is drawing to a close and you have not reached your goal or have prospects that have not been contacted. If you have made your decision as a part of a master plan, you have time to develop a good mail campaign at the least possible cost. If you don't, you will find that such a campaign is more costly, takes much longer that you expect, and the results will often be disappointing.

If you decide to use mail as a part of your overall strategy, you should consider securing professional help. This is especially true if you expect to use the mail to add to your donor base. Use "in-house" talent if the only mail contact will be purely follow-up on donors not contacted by individuals or in a phoneathon.

How Professionals Help

Professionals can help you in dozens of ways and will increase the effectiveness of your mail campaign. Securing external lists, writing copy, printing, and getting the material in the mail lead the list. People who specialize in direct-mail solicitation can save you money by preventing mistakes you would make in all of these areas. A mailing, even at nonprofit postal rates, to a list of 10,000 names can cost you $3000 to $5000 or more. If your copy and mailing package does not draw response, or your list is nonresponsive, you will not get enough in donations to cover the cost of the mailing. While a list of previous donors can generate response rates as high as 30 percent or more, external lists generally draw only a 0.5- to 3-percent response. A 2-percent response rate on a mailing of 10,000 would mean 200 donations. If the mailing cost you $5000, you would have to have an average gift of $25 from those responding to break even. An average gift from an external list is more likely to be $10 to $12. However, if you add 200 contributors to your files, additional mailings to these supporters over the next several years usually produce good results.

Therefore, if you plan to use direct mail to add to your donor base and use externally generated lists, you need sufficient money to hire professional help and do a first-class job in your promotional material.

If you decide to use professional help, start saving solicitations you receive in the mail almost every week. If you receive solicitations from local organizations, call them and find out who they used and how happy they were with the help. Contact professional firms listed in your yellow pages under "Advertising—Direct Mail," or "Mailing lists." Interview several companies and ask for samples of their work and a list of nonprofit clients they have served. Call these clients and discuss their experience with the company.

Developing and Maintaining Prospect Mailing Lists

You can develop good prospect lists from resources already available in your organization, and there are lists easily available, usually for a fee, from other sources. If you plan to start using direct mail to seek funds for your organization, remember to plan ahead. Developing a good list will cost money and time, and must be maintained or it will quickly become a burden rather than an asset.

Internal List Sources

Developing lists from within your own organization in most instances will produce the most productive list you will have. These names already identify with your organization because of previous contributions or some other involvement with your programs. This source also offers you several additional advantages. It is already your list. You don't have to pay anyone for the names. If your organization has kept good records over the years, it will be fairly accurate.

Current Members.   The best place to start is with the list of your current donors, board members, current clients or people who are using your services, and employees. Depending on the size of your organization and the nature of its work, this may be a sizable list to start with. For example, even small colleges often have several thousand alumni. They also have employees, parents of current and former students, and trustees. Organizations like the Boy Scouts and Girl Scouts often have thousands of current members and hundreds of volunteer leaders depending on the size of the community.

Additional Names from Donors.   Just as in the annual campaign, if asked, some of these people will provide names of friends, relatives, and associates that may have an interest in the work of your organization. If your organization has conducted campaigns in the past and has kept the campaign records, you have a list of people who helped you with a gift to that campaign but may not have made a gift in the past several years. Consider adding these people to your donor base by making an initial solicitation by mail.

Several years ago I was working with an organization that had conducted a fairly large capital campaign to build a camp. They had campaign records showing the name, address, and amount pledged. These names became a good source of prospects both for the annual campaign and for a special mail solicitation. One letter to an individual that had given $5000 to the capital campaign 6 years previously, got a response that included a check for $5000 for the annual campaign.

Previous Contacts.   Another source may be a list of past clients, program participants, or others that have benefited from services provided by your organization. For example, many colleges and universities have found that although they are not technically alumni, people that have taken a seminar or short course for personal enrichment can be effectively solicited for support to both annual campaigns and capital campaigns.

Vendors.   Companies and organizations that do business with your organization may also be good prospects. Who do you buy office supplies from? Who do you rent office space from? If your organization runs camping or recreational programs, who do you buy food, supplies, and equipment from? This list is easily retrievable from your organization's bookkeeper. Just ask for a list with names and addresses of those organizations you have purchased supplies or services from in the past several years. Current suppliers will be your best prospects.

Visitors and Guests.   Does your organization have a location or programs that attract visitors? A guest book asking for names and addresses will be a good source. Museums and art galleries often find this source effective. If you sell tickets to special performances, consider taking orders by phone and mailing the tickets to customers, keeping their names and addresses. If you have a major event, have a drawing for a door prize, and get names and addresses and even phone numbers that way.

Daily Contacts.   If you really want to generate names for mail solicitation, be aware of what your organization does on a daily basis in dealing with the public. You may get a lot of phone calls seeking information. Have a special brochure that explains your organization and with every call, suggest mailing the brochure to the caller. Another name is added to your list.

External List Sources

Once you have developed your internal list, you may want to consider external sources of additional names.

Exchange Lists.   One of the best sources is to exchange donor lists with other organizations in your community. This may take some careful communication with representatives of other organizations when you first start. It may even make you nervous. Do you want the other organization to contact your current donors for money for their organization? Do they want you contacting their donors? At first thought, you both may answer, no. However, there is little evidence to suggest that donors to your organization will leave you to support the other. Just the opposite is usually true. People that give to your organization probably are interested in other organizations that do good things in your community. People who give their money to nonprofit organizations generally give to several.

If you do agree to swap lists with another organization, a few tips to ensure good relationships: Make sure you are swapping lists of donors, not prospects. Agree in writing how each organization will use the list. Share material to be mailed to donors with each other. Agree that the list is to be used only once (perhaps with reminder mailings two or three times), and only when the person responds to the request for support does the name belong to the borrowing organization. With this understanding, if you are still concerned, seed your list with several names of employees and key board members. Ask these people to bring any mail requests for support to your attention. Spell the names incorrectly or change middle initials so you can know the source of the list. Note: Professional list owners do this when you rent a list to ensure that you are following the agreed upon contract.

List Brokers.   You can get excellent names through use of a list broker. These professionals work much like a real estate agent. They bring together the owner of a list and the organization needing the list. They receive a commission, usually 20 percent, from the owner of the list. As with a realtor, they are interested in keeping both parties happy with the transaction, so they can be very helpful to you. If you use a list broker, be sure to tell the broker exactly what you plan to do and what type person you believe will respond to your appeal. That way the broker can recommend a list for you. If there is not a mailing list broker in your community, you can get names of brokers from either the Mailing List Brokers Professional Association, 663 Fifth Avenue, New York, N.Y., 10022, or the National Council of Mailing List Brokers, 55 West 42nd Street, New York, N.Y., 10001.

List Owners.   It is possible to work directly with owners of lists. In your local community, you may find that the Chamber of Commerce will rent its list. More and more nonprofit organizations are renting their lists. Professional and trade associations may be a source as well.

If you consider working with list owners directly, make sure you have thought out your campaign carefully and know the characteristics of your current donors. A list of 100,000 names may be very nonresponsive if it is national in scope and your organization is identified with a local community. Unless you are very experienced in direct-mail solicitation, you will be better served by use of a list broker.

Compiled Lists.   As you explore direct-mail solicitation, sooner or later you will hear about compiled lists. There are two national organizations that compile lists, R. L. Polk Company and Donnelley Marketing. They build their lists primarily from automobile registrations and telephone directories, supplemented by driver's license information, city directory listings, and other data. Using a computer program, they integrate the names, addresses, and zip codes with census data related to income, sex, head of household, home ownership, etc., to produce lists that are called demographic lists. You can obtain names from these compiled sources to meet your needs. For example, you can rent names of all the people in your community that are home owners with an estimated annual income of $25,000 or more. The major problem with compiled lists is accuracy. Since about 25 percent of all Americans change residence each year, a significant percentage of your mail will be undeliverable.

Response Lists.   Usually when you work through a list broker, what you and the broker are seeking is a list of names of people that have responded to mail appeals. Lists of donors to charities are available. Lists of people that buy merchandise from direct mail are available. If your cause has some attraction to specialized audiences, you can get lists of subscribers to professional and trade magazines in these fields. The important principle to remember is that the names on the list have responded to some mailing in the past. These people are more apt to at least open and read your material.

Establishing and Maintaining Lists

Once you have decided that direct mail will be a part of your total annual fund raising efforts, you need to establish a system for maintaining and using your lists of names. To be successful with direct mail you must plan on mailing to the list several times a year. Be aware of the amount of time processing and recording responses will take. Except for very small organizations, sooner or later you will find yourself hampered with the time it takes to maintain an effective donor list for mail campaigns.

Manual Systems

If you are just starting out and your total list of names does not exceed approximately 1200 to 1500, you may be able to establish your initial system on index cards. You will need a place for name, address, city, zip, telephone number (if available), and probably a source code. Where did you get the name? Client, past board member, current officer, volunteer leader, vendor, past contributor, or similar classifications. A place for past giving records will be very helpful in the years ahead.

The cards can be filed alphabetically, and you may use colored tabs to designate special categories of contributors. If the cards are designed well, you can also use them to keep campaign records and other information, such as a notation that a thank you note was sent.

Two major problems will face you with such a manual system. When you are ready to mail, each name must be individually typed on an envelope and perhaps a pledge card. Once the envelopes have been typed and stuffed with the campaign material, they must be sorted by zip code if you are mailing at the nonprofit rate of postage. This adds additional time and effort to your campaign. When responses are received, posting by hand must be done, especially if you expect to continue to use the list for mail solicitation.

If you must use a manual system for your organization, one hint that will help: Keep your card file in alphabetical order at all times. When a donation is received, pull the card, note the contribution amount and date. Send the acknowledgment, and then file the card alphabetically in a "donors file." When it is time to do follow up mailings, address only those names remaining in the original file. Keep your two files separate. The next time you mail you may want to differentiate your appeal to past givers and to nonrespondents to earlier mailings.

Mechanical Systems

Your organization may have a mechanical addressing system currently in use that will aid you with direct mail fund raising. Addressograph and Scriptomatic are two systems still found in many organizations. These systems in some cases have some selectivity features, and they can be used to address envelopes and perhaps pledge cards. In most instances, follow the general guidelines for a manual system. You may find the address plates already filed alphabetically by zip code. If that is the case, you can run a set of index cards at the start of the campaign, manually sort them into an alphabetical file and proceed accordingly. Follow-up mailings may be a little more difficult. Many organizations using these systems find it easier to address all envelopes and "pull" contributors by comparing the givers file to the envelopes. Such systems can handle more names, but will reach their limit, depending on the system, at about 5000 names.

Computer Systems

The long-term answer for all organizations, and the immediate answer for organizations seeking to do direct mail campaigns to 5000 or more previous donors is the computer. In the past decade, the price of computers has dropped and capacity has expanded dramatically. In many instances relatively small lists can be handled with microcomputers with existing data-base software quite well. There are readily available data-base software programs that can handle 10,000 to 12,000 names. Once the names are in the computer, they can be sorted and resorted as needed. The names/records can be used to record gifts, acknowledgments, and the like. During campaign time, the files can be used to generate campaign reports on number of givers, total dollars contributed, and average size gift.

The same data file can be used throughout the year to send donors, and perhaps nondonors if you wish, newsletters and other related material from the organization. Usually these programs allow a good deal of flexibility in sorting and can often be used by the organization for other purposes. A number will, with the correct printer, address envelopes, pledge cards, and letters.

If your organization has more than 12,000 names currently or expects to grow to or beyond that number in the short term, you will want to consider special software programs designed for fund raising and direct-mail campaigns. These packages cost more than the data-base programs, and usually require a larger capacity microcomputer, a minicomputer, or perhaps a mainframe computer to operate. Consider contracting for such support with a data processing service company. In many instances the monthly fee will provide you a terminal in your office and either on-line service, where you can access your file at anytime, or a batch system that will run your files on the mainframe and deliver the reports and cards to you the next day.

If You Plan to Buy a Computer. While using computers to assist your organization in fund raising must be in your future plans, you should not rush into a decision or purchase the first system you see demonstrated. Strongly consider professional help in developing a long-range plan for supporting your fund-raising efforts with a computer. Design the ideal system with the features you feel you need before you discuss options with vendors. Look long and hard at software. Can it be modified to better suit your needs? Does the company provide ongoing support and upgrades? How long have they been in business? Will it actually work on the hardware you have or will buy? What is the total capacity in terms of individual contributor records the system can handle? How long would printing your entire list take?

Keep in mind three basic concepts throughout your search. Hardware (computers) only does what the software (programs) tells it to do. Hardware capacity is important, but it's only half the equation. Software has limits already set in its code. Altering these limits may be very expensive or impossible. Software that will do all that you want may cost much more than the hardware. Technology in hardware is changing so fast that even distributors have a hard time keeping up-to-date. It is a rare organization that does not upgrade both its hardware and its software within 3 to 5 years of installation. Long-term vendor reliability may be the most important factor in your decision.

Working with a List Broker

As noted earlier in this chapter, list brokers are professionals that bring together an owner of a list and a user of a list. They seek to keep both sides in the arrangement happy in the hopes of continued business and good reputation. You have the right to expect a broker, especially one that is a part of the National Association of List Brokers, to perform certain services as a part of the transaction.

What to Expect

A good broker has access to hundreds of response lists containing many thousands of names. He or she has an interest in getting you the best names for your solicitation and in using the lists provided by the owners of lists, who pay the commission. Since the broker spends full time in his or her profession, and has a better understanding of the types of lists available, he or she will attempt to match your needs with a list that has a good chance of response to causes such as yours. The broker will not guarantee the response rate, because there are too many variables that can change the results, including the copy, format, mailing package, the reputation of your organization, national and international events, and the like.

Read the Fine Print

When you rent a list, usually, the price is for a one-time use of the list. Under agreed upon conditions, it may be for use one or more times for follow-up mailings several weeks following the initial mailing. In these cases, expect the charges for using the list to be higher. To ensure themselves that you or others do not use the list more than the agreed upon usage, they seed the list with names that you cannot recognize. These individuals, upon receipt of solicitation material, send the material to the owner of the list who can trace the unauthorized mailing to your organization.

Normally, a simple contract for use of the list is submitted to you for approval. Read it carefully. If you don't understand any part of it or if you desire changes, your broker will secure the answers or modifications for you as a part of his or her service.

Individuals that respond to your solicitation become your names, and you are free to record the names and addresses in your records and continue to use the name in future mailings. Therefore, it is extremely important that you code your mailings to names on rented lists so that you can remember to record the name and address in your master file when the response arrives. You have paid a good deal of money for the name, so don't lose it through carelessness.

Using Your List Broker Effectively

Once you have selected a list broker, involve the broker in the early planning stages of your campaign. Tell the broker the type of person you believe will respond to your organization. Help the broker understand your organization and what you do in the community. The more the broker knows about your organization, the better the match between your needs and the list chosen.

A good broker is also experienced with postal regulations, mailing services, and ways to test lists. If you let the broker help the development of your campaign, you will get this advice as a part of the service.

Finally, a good broker will not consider the service complete until he or she helps you evaluate the results of the mailing. The broker is anxious to know what the response rate was, and any problems that you had with the mailing. Letting the broker help evaluate the mailing will give you the value of his or her experience, and may help you do an even better job in the future.

Large Lists. In some cases when you are renting a large number of names from a very large list, the information may be sent to the broker on magnetic tape for use by a local computer service bureau to address your mailing pieces. If your broker has been involved, this should cause no problems, as the broker will know this in advance and make sure that the proper equipment and service is available to you.

Testing Your List and Material

Once you have your list identified and your material sketched out, remember that you can test both the list and the presentation material. If you expect to do a major mailing, usually 50,000 or more pieces of mail, you should consider testing both the list and the package. If you are using a broker, he or she can help you secure a random sample of names from several lists so you can mail enough names to get the number of responses needed to fairly evaluate the differences between the lists.

Testing a List

To test a list, you need a sample of at least 5000 names from the list, randomly drawn so that they fairly represent the whole list. You want the names provided from each list to fairly represent the universe of the list.

Code your reply envelopes or devices so you can see which of the lists gave you the best response. *Caution:* make sure that the material sent out is exactly the same to the whole list, and that all the mailing is mailed the same day, preferably at the same hour at the same post office. Any variables that are different other than the source of the names will spoil the test.

Once you obtain the results of the mailing, usually about 4 weeks after the mail drop (the language used in direct mail to indicate the date you dropped the pieces in the mail), you can compare the results. Don't overreact to the results. Small differences in response rate are not meaningful. If one list gets a response rate of 1.2 percent and another 1.4 percent, you really don't have a statistically significant difference.

Testing Your Material

If you plan to make a very large mailing, you will also want to test your mailing package. Again using a random sample, mail to 10,000 names. This time you send 5000 of the list one letter and the other 5000 a second version of the letter. Through coding of the response card or envelope, track the differences in response.

In a similar fashion, you can test response devices, use of charge cards for example on one group and cash or pledges only on the other. You can test two color versus one color letters, window versus regular envelopes, and on and on. Don't go overboard on testing. The basic item that you will want to test is your appeal letter. Does it move people to action? Only those organizations that do huge amounts of direct-mail solicitation will have the time or money to test most other aspects of direct mail.

There do seem to be cycles in direct-mail fund-raising letters. One organization will try something new, and it will work very well. Others will jump on the train. Soon much of the material you receive will look much like the material you received from another organization last week, and you will get confused. Responses will drop off, and a new gimmick will emerge.

Understand Costs Before You Start

There are a lot of costs in direct-mail campaigns that you might overlook if you are not careful. Understand the total cost of a campaign and establish a budget before you start. Later you will want to compare your actual costs to your budget. If it is your first attempt, be prepared to do some estimating of costs. Do not try to tie down every figure to the penny for budgeting purposes.

Develop Estimates

To start the process, make some initial assumptions. How many pieces are you going to mail? If you are using your own list, you will know the figure. If you plan to rent a list, set a figure you believe will give you a fair chance to succeed, probably somewhere from 10,000 to 20,000. Remember, the fewer you mail, the higher cost per piece because of printing charges. The larger the printing run, the lower the cost per piece. However, you must be realistic. A 100,000 print run may have a very low per piece cost, but the postage is the same on a per piece basis.

The following is a list of items that you will usually pay for in a direct-mail campaign:

1. Copy and design, if you use professional help
2. Finished art, typesetting, and photographs
3. Mailing envelope
4. Letter
5. Brochure (if in addition to letter)

6. Response device

7. Reply envelope

8. Mailing services (inserting, affixing labels, sorting, and delivery to the post office)

9. List rental charge

10. Postage

A printer, after reviewing your proposed copy, can give you an estimate of costs per item printed, and usually will tell you options available that may save you money or may add more to your costs. For example, two-color runs cost more than one-color runs. Standard-size envelopes and paper will be cheaper than odd sizes. A mailing service will be able to quote you prices, usually on a per-thousand basis for stuffing, affixing labels, sorting, and delivering to the post office. Professional writers and layout artists will usually quote a price either for the finished job or per hour. These services may be provided by the printer. If the printer has in-house capability in these areas, it may be cheaper to get a package price from him. If he or she uses subcontractors, you may save money by contracting with professionals yourself and delivering the printer camera-ready art. If you go this way, make sure you know what specifications the printer will need to use your artwork and layouts.

Hidden costs.   There are also costs beyond the production and mailing that you must remember. First, if you use business reply envelopes (postage paid by you on return), you will have a cost per piece for each return. Second, you will have some processing costs you may want to consider. Processing the donation, sending a thank-you, and adding the name to your donor list for periodic contact all cost you money. You can probably estimate these costs if your organization has been operating for a few years.

How to Develop Your Initial Budget

Figure 10.1 is a budget sheet for direct mail. You can develop your own budget estimating form using this as a guide.

An Example.   Figure 10-2 shows the budget filled out with a hypothetical case. Let's look at what you can expect if the hypothetical example gets a 2% response rate.

XYZ ORGANIZATION DIRECT-MAIL BUDGET ESTIMATE

Date _____ Compiled by _____

Quantity to be mailed _____ Drop date _____

List source _____ Broker _____

	Estimate	Actual
1. Cost of mailing:		
2. Copy/design	$_____	_____
3. Finished art/typesetting and photos	$_____	_____
4. Mailing envelope	$_____	_____
5. Letter	$_____	_____
6. Brochure	$_____	_____
7. Reply device	$_____	_____
8. Return envelope	$_____	_____
9. Mailing service $_____ per M × _____ M =	$_____	_____
10. List rental $_____ per M × _____ M =	$_____	_____
11. Postage: _____ pcs at $_____ per piece	$_____	_____
12. Subtotal (Lines 2–11)	$_____	_____
13. Cost per 1000 pieces mailed (Line 12 / _____ M)	$_____	_____

14. Response processing: (per piece)
  (Est. response rate _____ %) _____
  pieces _____		

15. Postage _____ at _____ per	$_____	_____
16. Acknowledgment _____ at _____ per	$_____	_____
17. *Address corrections _____ at _____ per	$_____	_____
18. Processing costs _____ at _____ per	$_____	_____
19. Subtotal (Lines 15–18)	$_____	_____
20. Cost per piece for responses Line 19 / Line 14)	$_____	_____
21. Total cost per 1000 pieces mailed (Line 12 + Line 19)	$_____	_____

Figure 10.1. Direct mail budget sheet

Figure 10.1. (*Continued*)

22. Estimated average donation	$_____ _____
23. Estimated average net donation (Line 22 − Line 20)	$_____ _____
24. Number of average net donations to breakeven: (Line 21 / Line 23)	_____ _____
25. Response rate of list at breakeven: (Line 24 / Total mailed)	_____ _____

* Use only on mailings to your own previous donor list.

You will get 400 responses with an average net contribution of $13.50. Four hundred times $13.50 equals $5400. Your total costs for the mailing and processing came to $7340, giving you a net loss of $1940. Results like this would be fairly typical for an initial mailing using a rented list with a response rate of 2%. Even if you overlook your processing costs of $1.50 per response and you do not acknowledge the gifts, you still have a loss of $1220.

If you are going to raise money by direct mail, do not expect your initial mailing to breakeven. At best, the names you mail to are prospects. Look at what you gain, 400 new donors at an average of $13.50. Since donors normally respond with a contribution for several years, your donor list will expand, bringing you a "profit" on subsequent solicitations. Response rates from your donor list can easily run 20 percent. If you can develop a donor list of 20,000 names from prospect mailings over the years, you can secure significant funding by mail.

As you will note in Figure 10.1, there is also a column called "Actual," so you can track your campaign and have a permanent record of how well your mailing did. Keeping such a record will assist you greatly in planning future campaigns.

Long-term Implications

If you are going to start using mail campaigns on a regular basis, you need to look at the long-term implications. Even though you may lose a few thousand dollars on your first try, remember, you have picked up 300 to 400 new donors to your organization. If you used a rented list, these names are now yours. Put them on your in-house donor list for future solicitation. You may include them in your regular annual campaign for the next campaign, especially if they gave a gift signifi-

XYZ ORGANIZATION DIRECT-MAIL BUDGET ESTIMATE

Date 10/15/XX   Compiled by S. Jones

Quantity to be mailed 20 M   Drop date 3/15/XX

List source ABC Company   Broker J. Brown

1.	Cost of mailing:	
2.	Copy/design	$ 800.00
3.	Finished art/typesetting and photos	$ 500.00
4.	Mailing envelope	$ 600.00
5.	Letter	$ 500.00
6.	Brochure	$ 500.00
7.	Reply device	$ 320.00
8.	Return envelope	$ 320.00
9.	Mailing service $ 20 per M × 20 M =	$ 400.00
10.	List rental $ 45 per M × 20 M =	$ 900.00
11.	Postage: 20 M pcs at .085 per piece	$1,700.00
12.	Subtotal (Lines 2–11)	$6,540.00
13.	Cost per 1000 pieces mailed (Line 12 /20 M)	$ 327
14.	Response processing: (per piece) (Est. response rate 2 %)	400 pieces
15.	Postage 400 at .27 per	$ 108.00
16.	Acknowledgement 400 at .30 per	$ 120.00
17.	Address corrections ___ at ___ per	$ ___
18.	Processing costs 400 at 1.50 per	$ 600.00
19.	Subtotal (Lines 15–18)	$ 828.00
20.	Cost per piece for responses (Line 19 / Line 14)	$ 2.07
21.	Total cost for 20 M pieces mailed (Line 12 + Line 19)	$7,368.00
22.	Estimated average donation	$ 13.50
23.	Estimated average net donation (Line 22 − Line 20)	$ 11.43
24.	Number of average net donations to breakeven: (Line 21 / Line 23)	645
25.	Response rate of list at breakeven: (Line 24 / Total mailed) 641/20,000 =	3.2%

Figure 10.2. Direct mail example budget

cantly above your average-size gift and further research indicates that they should be included in your annual campaign for personal contact.

Contributors will continue to support your organization by mail if they feel that their gifts were appreciated and used for a good cause. That's why acknowledgments and newsletters are important. Experts in direct mail suggest that a "typical" donor secured through mail solicitation will donate about $150 to a nonprofit organization over the years. If you can add 400 new donor names a year, each year's additions should generate about $60,000 in operating income over the lifetime of their giving.

Even when the donor from a previous year does not respond, do not throw the name out of your files. Many organizations have found that it is productive to maintain the names in the donor file for 3 years. Such a person, during this period, would be solicited from 10 to 20 times by mail. Some people may have intended to send another contribution, but your request reached them just as a child was getting married, or the car was in the shop for major repairs, and they just put off making the contribution. Several mailings per year are common if you expect to raise much money with direct mail.

Telling Your Story by Mail

Some week, analyze the mail you get. If you are like the average American you will get between 5 and 15 pieces of mail seeking to sell you some product or service or ask you to send a donation. What do you do with this mail? You, like most people, probably call it "junk mail." Many of the pieces you may not even open! Others you will open, glance at, and discard. A few pieces you will open and read. Fewer still will cause you to take some action. You may save the piece for later review. It may be a catalog of gift items you can order. If you have a friend with a birthday coming up, you may choose an item and order it. Today, you may even order it using a toll-free telephone number staffed 24 hours a day. If the request is for a donation and you are motivated to help, you may save it until you write your checks out at the end of the month, or you may respond immediately with a check or pledge. If that's the way you respond to mail solicitation, you are like most Americans.

What can fund raisers learn from this? When you are attempting to secure donors by use of response lists secured from outside sources, remember that many people that receive your solicitation will throw it away without opening it. Of those that do, many will quickly discard it. Only a very few will read your material very carefully and respond with a gift. Keep this in mind as you start to develop your material for your campaign. Your first challenge is to get the person to open your envelope, and the second is to get them to read beyond the first line or two!

If you are now humble enough, let's look at the key factors to keep in mind when you develop your presentation to the prospect.

Write to a Friend

You will probably do a better job if you start with your basic presentation piece, the letter requesting support. It must deliver the message, ask for the gift, and respond to questions the potential donor may have in place of a volunteer solicitor.

Before you start your copy, get a mental picture of what you believe is a typical donor to your organization. What are his or her concerns and values? What would make the person respond with a gift? How old is the person in your mind? What does he or she do for a living? How does the person feel about his or her community? With this mental picture in your mind, write a letter to that person, telling him or her, who you are, what you want, and why the person should care.

Start with a 2 × 4 Statement

Remember the old joke about the farmer who was seen hitting the mule over the head before beginning to plow? When asked why, the farmer responded, "if you want a mule to listen to you, first you have to get its attention!" Your opening sentence must get the reader's attention. If it doesn't, the reader may well stop at that point. You have only a few seconds of the person's time to get him or her to continue reading.

You will have to make the copy fit your organization and its purpose, but you need a dramatic opening statement. "Last week, over 2000 children in our community went to bed hungry!" or "Do you remember playing 'stick ball' in the street when you were growing up?" or "I believe you are a person that is concerned about _____" are examples of 2 × 4 statements.

Give Compelling Reasons

Follow with compelling reasons why the person reading the letter should help. For example, "Governmental support that has been helping with the problem has decreased recently. Our city does not have adequate recreational facilities for our young people. There is not enough professional help for the people in our community that need it now."

Ask for a Gift

Suggest an amount. This is a must. Let the person know how much it costs to get something done about the problem. "Fifty dollars will make it possible for a young child to spend a week in our camp this summer instead of hanging out on a street corner." "Twenty-five dollars will help us feed a hungry person for a week." "Your gift of $_____ will make it possible for us to _____." Most organizations will be much more effective with mail appeals seeking help to accomplish some special project, rather than seeking help to pay the operating costs of the organization. Since your organization is providing some service to your community, single out some special project or service and help the reader identify with that aspect of your work.

Offer Something in Return

Tell the reader you will send him or her a quarterly newsletter telling of the progress your organization is making. Some organizations actually offer some premium. For example: "When we receive your gift, we will send you a bookmark made by one of our patients to thank you and remind you daily of the help you have been in aiding these handicapped people." Your organization will need to decide if such a premium is appropriate. Most nonprofit organizations do not offer premiums, but certificates of membership, newsletter subscriptions, or "hot line" access numbers for assistance by your organization can be considered.

Ask for Action

Close your letter by asking for an immediate response, such as "Your check in the enclosed envelope will help us treat a sick child next week."

The letter should be signed by someone with name recognition if possible—the chairperson of your board of trustees, the president of your organization, etc. The letter should be on some type of letterhead, perhaps developed for the campaign. Listing the names of the board of directors can help build credibility. Perhaps a picture of a person your organization has helped printed in the upper corner can help.

The signature, even though it is printed on, should be in blue ink to give the appearance of a signature. Some research also suggests that a P.S. improves response. If you use one, print it to look like a hand written post script, in the same color ink as the signature. Why does this work? I don't know, but research suggests that this is the first thing the reader sees! The P.S. should be action oriented: "Your gift may save a life!"

Make It Easy to Respond

Include a return envelope so that the reader will not have to address it. There is a difference of opinion on whether it should be postage paid or whether you should ask the person to place a stamp on it. If you want to encourage pledges, also include a pledge card. The card will be similar to the pledge card you use in your regular campaign. Have a signature block, a statement about the pledge, and a place to check off the size of the gift. This reinforces the asking for a specific amount. It is a subtle way to suggest higher giving levels. More and more organizations are letting donors give through use of a bank credit card. You might want to consider this.

What Works Best?

The debate goes on about many issues in direct mail. Should you use window envelopes or not? Should you use computer-addressed labels on the envelope? Should you include a brochure? Should you put copy on the outer envelope? One color, two color, or more? Type of paper, size of paper, color of paper, and premiums. There are no simple, clear answers. Remember that you walk a very thin line between being seen as too extravagant (slick paper/multicolor) and too amateurish. If you are planning far enough ahead, you can test your copy and other features of your campaign. If you plan to make direct mail an ongoing event, and a major source of income, be prepared to test your lists, mailing packages, and message.

When and How Often Should You Mail?

Nonprofit organizations using a great deal of direct mail to raise operating dollars have found that some months are better than others. The type of organization also seems to make a difference. Alumni associations have different experiences with mail campaigns as compared to other organizations.

Best Time to Mail?

There are no clear answers to this question. If you are mailing to previous donors, November seems to be a good month for many organizations. First, it is the season for sharing and being thankful for what you have. Second, the individual's tax year is about to end, and a gift to your organization is deductible. Some organizations have found

April and May to be good months, perhaps because income tax refund checks are being received and many people see this return as found money, and share it with others.

If you are using direct mail as a follow-up to contact previous donors that were not called on in your annual campaign, you will probably be mailing in April and May. If you are using direct mail as a major segment of your annual campaign, you will be able to plan different mailing schedules.

How Soon Will You Get Results?

After you put your mailing in the post office, you will begin getting results in about 7 to 10 days. The responses will increase, and by the end of the third week after you drop, about 21 days, you will peak. You will probably have most responses by the end of 6 weeks. A few will trickle in as people find your request in a pile of mail they have put aside, but it won't be many.

Repeat the Mailing?

If you can afford to, the answer is yes, especially to donor lists. Remember that direct mail is similar to advertising. You may see several hundred advertisements during the week without any conscious awareness, but when you need a product you seem to see more ads for that product. Direct mail is the same way. Your first piece may be discarded or misplaced, and a second mailing will produce a response. Most professionals suggest that your donor list can be mailed once every 6 weeks for three mailings to gain the maximum response rate from the list. Prospect mailings (nonprevious donors) can be remailed from time to time if you can afford it.

Sometimes a list can improve as the prospects get more and more knowledge of your organization. Keep in mind that a donor is likely to repeat a donation within 4 or 5 years, so careful cultivation by mail calls for patience and perseverance.

If You Want to Give It a Try

A good way to start your initial effort in raising money with mail solicitation is to use your own list of current donors as noted earlier. Many organizations have donor bases that they find it difficult to contact through individual solicitation during the annual campaign. A list of donors that have already supported you, even at a modest level, can become the start of a mail campaign. Since larger gifts should receive personal solicitation, you want to use only those prospects that give relatively small contributions, so you can use your volunteers to contact the prospects with higher potential for support.

You of course have to define what modest levels are for your organization, but the level is such that the cost of handling the mail solicitation and the annual servicing of the membership (acknowledgment of the gift, mailing of periodic newsletters, and administrative costs associated with keeping the person's file) must exceed the size of the gift, or you are losing money soliciting this individual.

Select Your Best "Mail" Prospects

First of all, review your current list of contributors. What is the average size gift for the entire list? (Total dollars raised divided by the number of individual gifts). If you had one or two unusually large gifts that you don't expect to be repeated annually, you should delete these gifts before your calculations. If your organization is typical of most others you will find that about 20 percent of your gifts provide about 80 percent of your total dollars, and the remaining 80 percent of your contributors provide only 20 percent of your dollars. If you know this information, you can calculate the average-size gift from those contributors that provide you regular but small gifts. In many organizations, this will probably average out to gifts ranging from $15 to $50 per year.

Take the names of the 20 percent of your givers and develop the traditional personal solicitation campaign. Use direct mail for the 80 percent. As soon as a donor passes the $75 contribution, move him or her into the traditional campaign the following year.

Develop Your Presentation

Once you have identified the names you plan to solicit by mail, you are ready to plan your mail campaign. Your contact by mail should be directed as far as possible to the individual who receives it. For example, if your list is of previous givers, refer to that fact in the letter. Draft your first attempt with a specific individual in mind. Make it your personal note to him or her thanking him or her for their past support, telling him or her what you have accomplished with the past gift and asking the person to renew his or her support for the current year. Just as in a face-to-face solicitation, suggest a gift size. Ask for a decision now, and make it as easy as possible to act. Enclose a reply envelope and a pledge card. Have suggested giving levels listed so a check mark is all that is needed. Offer the option of billing by the organization on a cycle selected by the individual.

Drop It

Not the project, the mailing. Mail your presentation to the list and trace the responses carefully. How many responses the first 7 to 10 days? When did it peak out? Average size gift? Method of payment? Total results of the effort? Did you cover the cost of the mailing? What did you learn?

11

Raising Money through Planned Giving

"John, if I could show you a way that you could increase your retirement income, reduce your estate taxes, give you a tax deduction on your income tax obligation this year, and make it possible for you to make a major gift to our hospital that would continue its work in the treatment of cancer patients that you have supported in the past, would you be interested?"

Such a conversation happens daily between planned giving officers and individuals throughout America. Planned giving, previously called deferred giving, is one of the dramatically expanding components of securing funding for nonprofit organizations.

Most people who make major gifts to nonprofit organizations do so as a part of a financial plan developed in cooperation with their personal tax advisors and representatives of a tax-exempt institution. Most are senior citizens, and this segment of our society is growing rapidly; therefore, prospects for planned gifts are increasingly available to most organizations.

Federal tax laws passed in 1969 greatly expanded opportunities for nonprofit organizations by providing tax incentives for individuals to make charitable gifts during their lifetime while retaining some benefits from those resources until their death or the death of other loved ones. This change in the law broadened the concept of deferred gifts to planned gifts, and has worked to the great advantage of nonprofit organizations throughout America. The number of bequests has been on the rise for the past 20 or more years, and in 1985 reached $5.18 billion, reflecting a 6.5 percent increase over 1984.

Establishing a Planned Gifts Program

Planned giving programs are not appropriate for every nonprofit organization. Any organization seeking endowments and sizable gifts to perpetuate its work must have a significant history of performance that warrants such support. Planned giving programs require a lot of time and effort for a number of years before sizable benefits to your organization will be realized. Unless you are large enough and strong enough to sustain an ongoing program of donor cultivation, it is best to establish your ability to raise annual funds for your program and establish your worth to your community before attempting to secure planned gifts.

Understanding Planned Giving

All too often, when you begin to consider establishing a planned giving program, you find material that seems complex, legalistic in language, and difficult to understand. While the technicalities are hard to understand and require legal assistance, you do not need to be a lawyer or accountant to grasp the idea and begin the development of a planned giving program for your organization.

Keep several thoughts in mind: (1) no two gifts are structured exactly alike. Each is custom designed for the donor with the advice of his or her attorney, accountant, and perhaps financial planner. (2) Both federal and state law affects the gift and competent legal counsel is a must in making such a gift. (3) Your job is to bring a prospect with a deep commitment to your program and sufficient resources to make a gift and his or her attorney and other advisors together to discuss a gift to your organization.

Basic Planned Gift Techniques

There are several ways someone can give you a gift. Some will be called deferred because they do not actually get passed to you or are available for your use until the death of the donor or other beneficiaries designated. Other gifts bring you annual income immediately, but the gift reverts to the donor or beneficiaries at some time specified in the gift instrument. While you don't have to know all of the details of each technique, a brief description will help you understand an individual's many options in planned giving.

Bequests and Devises under a Will

A gift can be made through the will of an individual. Subject to certain limitations, anyone can leave property to any person or organization. It may be a fixed amount or a percentage of the assets of the probated estate. It can be a gift of cash, securities, or property. Your organization may or may not know about the bequest or devise. You will know only if the writer of the will tells you. Assuming legal competency, a will can be changed at any time; therefore, a gift under a will is not reality until the death of the donor and the probate of the will is completed.

Although donors can change their wills at any time, most do not if they made the commitment to themselves at the time of the writing of the will and they have a genuine interest in the work your organization has done and will continue to do.

Gifts of Property

Some gifts of property may come to you through a will. Under certain conditions, donors can give you property while they are alive, retain the right to use the property during their lifetime and that of a spouse or some other beneficiary, and get some tax benefits for making the gift. Care must be taken to meet all conditions prescribed under current tax law.

A gift of property, real estate or personal property such as art works, may generate reductions in income tax that would be due if the donor sold the property. Reduction in estate tax could also result from the gift of property to charity.

There are complex regulations drawn by the Internal Revenue Service and perhaps state agencies concerning gifts of property. These regulations should be checked carefully by both the donor and the organization prior to completion of the gift.

Charitable Remainder Trusts

A donor that owns appreciated property and faces the payment of income tax upon sale of the property may find it advantageous to give the property to you, rather than sell it, and receive a charitable deduction for income tax purposes. Furthermore, the donor could keep the income from the property during his or her lifetime and the lifetime of a spouse or other beneficiary. If the property is not generating much income and is saleable, you could sell the gifted property and reinvest the proceeds in an asset which produces a higher income. Thus, the donor could actually increase his or her annual income, not pay tax on sale of the property, and obtain an income tax deduction.

There are two basic types of charitable remainder trusts:

Charitable Remainder Unitrusts.   The donor receives annual income based on a fixed percentage of the trust assets. The amount paid to the donor will change from year to year as the value of the trust assets change. Current law requires that the payout to the donor be at least 5 percent annually, but it can be more. At the death of the donor and any designated beneficiaries, the value of the trust goes to the nonprofit organization.

Charitable Remainder Annuity Trusts.   These trusts are like the unitrusts except that the donor will receive a fixed dollar amount each year. The amount will not change from year to year. If the trust earns more than the amount paid to the donor, the excess is added to the principal of the trust. If the trust does not earn enough to meet the fixed payments, the balance needed is taken from the principal.

Charitable Gift Annuity

A donor can give you an irrevocable gift of money or property, and be paid a fixed dollar amount each year for his or her lifetime. A portion of the annual payment to the donor is considered to be a return of principal and is therefore not taxable income. The assets of your organization back this annuity, not just the donor's gift. As with other techniques an annuity can be paid to both the donor and spouse for their lifetimes. Unlike some other planning devices, the annuity can be paid only on a maximum of two lives.

The annuity is normally easier to write and is helpful to smaller donors. It is different from a charitable remainder annuity trust.

Pooled Income Funds

Pooled income funds are attractive because they can be utilized by smaller donors. Your organization must be qualified by the Internal Revenue Code to establish a pooled income fund. Requirements are complex, and you should seek legal assistance and review the IRS requirements carefully before attempting to establish such a fund. Gifts from donors are placed in this fund and managed by your organization.

Each donor to the fund receives a share of the earnings based in proportion to the value of their contribution. The donor receives an income tax deduction (if he or she itemizes deductions) the year the gift is made.

Charitable Lead Trust

This trust is different from those discussed above. This trust pays your organization income earned on the trust assets for the term of the trust and then the principal is returned to the donor or a designated noncharitable beneficiary. The payout to you can be a fixed annual amount or a fixed percentage determined each year. Generally, the donor receives a charitable contributions deduction for the present value of the payments the charity is to receive over the term of the trust.

Gifts of Life Insurance

The gift of life insurance is a popular means for donors to make a major contribution to a favorite charity and receive the benefit of an income tax deduction for the annual premium. There are a number of ways to structure the gift of life insurance. Generally, the key is for your organization to become the owner of the policy through an irrevocable assignment. The donor then gifts the premium amounts at least annually to you and you pay the premiums. The donor takes the income tax deduction of the annual amount gifted to you.

At the death of the donor, you collect the face value of the policy. During the lifetime of the donor you can borrow the cash value if desired. This makes it possible for you to pay the premium if the donor decides to stop gifting premium amounts, or you can take "paid up" insurance and cease payments of annual premiums.

The donor could make the gift by buying a "single premium" policy naming your organization as the owner and beneficiary. At the death of the donor, you will receive the face amount of the policy. The donor gets the premium paid as a tax deduction.

The dramatic opportunity for your organization with life insurance lies with the simplicity in the mechanics of the gift. No complex trust management is necessary. The bookkeeping is simple. If the policy is not given to you paid in full, the premium notices come to you as owner of the policy. You pay the premium and bill the donor for the premium amount. Donors with fairly small assets can make significant gifts through the use of life insurance.

Benefits of Planned Giving

As you can see, there are benefits for both donors and your organization. Although no two gifts are exactly alike, the benefits are explainable to prospects in simple terms, and the details can be worked out with expert assistance. The donor and your organization will know *before* the gift the full details and its financial impact on both parties.

Benefits for the Donor

Donors receive several benefits from planning gifts to charitable organizations.

1. The donor gets the satisfaction that comes from helping support an organization that is or has been important to him or her.

2. The donor gets the personal recognition that is important to many people.

3. The donor can establish his or her personal "place in history" by helping your organization continue its work after the donor is dead.

4. The donor can reduce the impact of federal income and estate taxes. In some cases, state death and income taxes could also be reduced.

5. It is also possible the donor can improve personal income during his or her life and the life of a spouse or other beneficiary.

Benefits for the Organization

Your organization can also receive some important benefits through planned giving.

1. You can secure long-term funding, especially for endowment purposes.

2. You can secure substantial gifts that may not be available to you any other way.

3. You will get donors through planned giving programs that will become annual supporters in addition to their major gift. If they make

a major gift to you, they will know a great deal about your work and will be excited about what you accomplish each year.

4. They become outstanding "role models" for others related to your organization, and may lead you to more major gifts.

Ten Steps to Establish a Planned Giving Program

You can establish a planned giving program if you are willing to make an initial investment in people and material. You *must* keep in mind that developing a planned giving program takes time. You will not see an immediate payoff. Cultivation takes a lot of time and patience. Many of the gifts you receive will come as a surprise. While most fund-raising professionals expect to be evaluated on performance and the ability to reach clearly defined goals, you will not be able to measure results this way in planned giving programs. A staff member working on planned giving may make a visit that results in a bequest or devise in a board member's will that does not become known to you for 10 years. That staff member may have moved to new employment long before the actual gift is received.

As with other campaigns you organize each year, planned giving campaigns take similar organizational skills, quality leadership, board commitment, and careful execution. Whereas a capital campaign or annual campaign is a relatively short, intensive effort, a planned giving campaign really has no end. It calls for patience and persistence.

At this stage of the process you should consider professional advice. Hire a consultant experienced in planned giving. You are laying the foundation that can bring you millions of dollars over the years, and you need to start on a sound footing. A lot of help is available, and a good consultant can help you establish and launch a solid effort that will have long-term benefits.

Step 1—Secure Board Understanding and Commitment

The idea of planned giving will be new to most of your board. You will need to educate the members on the potential, principles involved, and the mechanics of getting started. This will take more than a single presentation at a board meeting. If you want to succeed, it will take not only their understanding, but their commitment evidenced by their involvement through making deferred or planned gifts personally.

Step 2—Appoint a Planned Giving Committee

Planned giving will need a standing committee of the board. The chairperson must have the same qualities of respect and leadership skill as called for in your annual campaign. The chairperson will be responsible for helping recruit a committee and keeping the committee active and supportive if you are to succeed.

As in your annual campaign, you should expect the chairperson and the members of the committee to make a personal commitment before they ask others to consider a gift. Not all members of the committee need to be extremely wealthy. Bequests or devises in a will, gifts of life insurance, or gifts to a trust fund will make it possible for almost everyone to support your effort.

You will want at least one attorney and one accountant on the committee who are members of the board if possible. The entire committee should not be made up of attorneys and accountants, however. Members should include influential community leaders, former officers of the board, leadership identified in your annual campaign or capital campaign, and even a few of your long-time volunteers.

While the attorney on your committee will prove invaluable in the organizational phases of setting up a planned giving program, it is unfair to expect him or her to provide the legal services that will be needed when you are negotiating significant gifts. You will need to be prepared to hire legal counsel to represent your organization when this time comes.

Step 3—Adopt Basic Policies and a Budget

Basic policies need to be approved by the board. If you are going to set up a pooled income fund, the details of this application must be worked out. You will want to consider policies on the type of gifts you will seek, minimum gifts for certain type trusts, who is authorized to negotiate for gifts, confidentiality of information, and anticipated use of funds received.

You will eventually need an investment advisory committee and some policy guidelines for this committee. State and federal laws may require you to file certain documents with the state before you start.

A budget must be developed and approved. Are you going to use a consultant? Will a staff member be employed to lead the effort? You will need money for travel, training, direct mail, office space, legal fees, and general office support. While you may find it acceptable and feasible to start with a part-time employee leading this effort, even this person must have the basic support to succeed.

Step 4—Train the Board and Staff

Like the annual campaign, the board and staff need to know about the program and how it works. Everyone on the board and all staff must know that you are seeking gifts through the use of planned giving techniques. They must know who to refer interested people to. They will be much more effective in recognizing interest in people if they understand the principles involved.

Since many of your initial prospects for your planned giving program will come from the board and staff, this training will be important to the cultivation of these people. You will be asking these people to suggest the names of friends and associates for follow-up by your planned giving committee.

Step 5—Develop a Marketing Plan

You will need a plan to educate your constituency, attorneys, accountants, financial planners, and bank trust officers in your community, about the work of your organization and its need for significant gifts using wills, trusts, insurance, and related instruments.

Much of your early effort will be educating your constituency on the basics of planned giving. Much of this can be done successfully with direct mail. Material is readily available from commercial sources, but you must be prepared to systematically keep this mail program going.

You will develop special editions of your case statement (see Chapter 3) and related support materials for promotional efforts. Seminars and special events designed to expose people to the concept of wills, bequests, trusts, and related matters will be important.

Careful cultivation and personal visits by members of your staff or your planned giving committee will be necessary. This will take careful planning and a follow-up mechanism to make sure that those interested hear from you on a regular basis.

Step 6—Develop a Prospect List

Like other campaigns, you must have a prospect list. This list is best drawn in the early stages from your board and others deeply involved in the work of your organization. From there it can expand as fast as you have resources to allocate to this function.

Use the basic principles of prospect identification and evaluation discussed in Chapters 1 and 4. You can use the Potential Prospect Form, Figure 1.1 from Chapter 1, as a beginning point.

You will want to do much more in-depth prospect research for your planned giving program. The more you know about the prospect and his or her interest, the better you will be able to help them and your organization plan a major gift. Prospecting is most often a staff function.

Step 7—Launch Your Direct Mail Cultivation

As an initial step, use direct mail to educate and inform your initial prospects of your interest in helping them with their financial planning. You will want these mailings to offer educational programs on the need for a will and estate planning as a service to the prospect with no obligation on their part. This is the first step in careful and consistent cultivation of your prospects.

Personal letters, signed by a key leader in your organization and enclosing a brochure about the concept of planned giving are a good start. You can print your own material or use commercially available supplies and have your name printed on the brochures. Such subjects as: "The Importance of a Will," "A Confidential Record of Personal Financial Plans," or "Tax Benefits of Establishing a Trust," illustrate the kind of material you will be using.

Step 8—Start a Series of Seminars

One of the best ways to get your program off to a running start is to conduct a series of seminars for your prospects on writing a will, planning an estate, how to make a substantial gift to a favorite charity, or how to improve retirement. Use attorneys, accountants, bank trust officers, insurance agents, and personal financial planners for these seminars. Often they will donate their time for these presentations. If you don't know anyone like this and members of your planned giving committee don't either, contact other nonprofit organizations in your community and find out what they are doing with planned giving and get suggestions from them.

Remember that you are cultivating prospects. Do not let people who help with these seminars take advantage of the situation and solicit business from your guests. Make this clear to all you ask to make a presentation before you invite them to help you.

Step 9—Start Cultivation Visits

At your seminars and through your mailings you will begin getting the names of people that want a personal visit. Start planning these visits. Schedule them at the convenience of the prospect. In many cases they will be in the home of the prospect. They may be in the evening or on weekends. You *must* be prepared to make visits to the prospect over a period of time. These visits are not like an annual campaign call where you will be asking for a gift at the visit. It may take weeks, months, and maybe years to get to the gift stage. Be patient. Would you expect to give a gift of a million dollars to some organization with an initial visit?

Be prepared to answer questions. The prospect may want to know more about your work, but will most likely want to know what your long-term needs are and how a gift would help. If they are seeking to improve their income and that of a spouse you will be helping two concerned people understand how a gift to your organization will be structured. Be patient, be prepared to return several times, and most of all, keep the needs of the donor your primary consideration.

Step 10—Ask for Gifts

At some point you will need to suggest a gift to your organization. Cordial and sympathetic approaches work best. You must communicate your interest in the needs of the donor. "Do you think it is time to consider a gift to a trust fund that would guarantee you and your spouse income for the rest of your lives?" illustrates one possible approach.

Offer to arrange, at your expense in some cases, appointments with an attorney or other advisor if the person has no preference. Provide the prospective donor a list of questions he or she will want to discuss in private with their attorney or tax advisor. Offer transportation or other resources if that will help.

Most of all, be patient, supportive and empathetic. The person may make a substantial gift to your organization, and such a decision requires your best efforts and support.

Office Support Systems

When you start a planned gifts program, make sure that you have the support systems and policies in place. Accurate record keeping is important. Confidentiality must be assured. Acknowledging gifts, prompt response for requests for help or information must be done quickly. If you are using part-time help, don't fall into the trap of taking messages for this person that may not be delivered for several days.

Have someone in your office trained to handle mail or telephone contacts from these prospects. Have all office personnel trained to know when such a contact is being made. This is not easy and will take continual orientation of employees.

Develop appropriate recognition for donors. A special place in your office with recognition plaques is a start. However, don't use public recognition without the prior approval of the donor. Make sure your board officers know of all gifts. The donor may well know one or more of your officers and would expect that they would know and personally acknowledge the gift.

Be ready to continue to support your planned giving for a long time. Try to employ or assign staff to this effort that are likely to be with you for the foreseeable future. Consistency in your approach may be one of the most important things you do in planned giving.

Annually evaluate your program. Make sure your systems are working and your direct mail program is on schedule. If the staff member assigned has this as an additional duty, evaluate the number of prospect visits made and the number of prospects added to the cultivation list. It is easy to launch a good program and let it fall into a state of nonuse if you are not careful. Give your planned giving chairperson a chance to give a report to the board. Make success in planned giving a part of your annual report to your constituency and, above all, be patient!

12

Raising Money through a Capital Campaign

What Is a Capital Campaign?

A capital campaign is seeking money to accomplish objectives that are in addition to or beyond the normal activities of your organization and its annual operating budget. It is usually a campaign to raise relatively large amounts of money to build or add to existing physical facilities, build an endowment, purchase land, buy major equipment, or establish new or unique services not currently provided.

Climate for Successful Campaigns

Only those organizations that have established a regular base of annual support and a reputation within the community for offering services of value should consider conducting a capital campaign. You will need very large gifts from wealthy people and organizations and you will be involving many more volunteers in the campaign than you normally use in your annual campaign. For most organizations, a capital campaign is conducted no more often than every 10 years. In recent years, some religious groups, educational institutions, and medical facilities have conducted capital campaigns on a more frequent basis, but the number of successful capital campaigns following this pattern are still the exception, not the rule.

In some communities you may find a formal or informal review and approval process facing your organization if you decide to conduct a capital campaign. The United Way in most major communities initiates such a process with the tacit encouragement of major donors, corporations, and foundations in the community. If your organization is affiliated with the United Way, formal approval to conduct a capital campaign may be a part of your participation agreement.

There are good reasons for such a screening function, regardless of whether or not you are required to review your plans with a community group. All capital campaigns are built upon the need for large contributions from a few wealthy sources in the community. Every community, no matter how big, has only a few such sources. If, for example, a local university, a hospital, and a large community agency are currently conducting a capital campaign or have recently completed such a campaign, you may find that the wealthy donors that are critical to your success are unwilling or unable to give a gift to your campaign now. While few large communities will ever have an open time during any year when no nonprofit organization is seeking capital funds, you must know what the market conditions are before you launch such a campaign or you may fail despite your best efforts and outstanding leadership.

The Four Key Differences

A capital campaign differs from an annual campaign in four areas: the purpose of the funds solicited, the size of the campaign goal, the length of the campaign, and the planning and preparation needed to conduct a successful campaign.

The basic principles outlined in Chapter 3 and discussed in more detail in Chapters 4 and 5, remain the same. You will still be utilizing trained volunteers asking peers for gifts to your campaign. Top-quality campaign leadership is still the key ingredient to success, and the results will reflect your ability to organize, train, and motivate volunteers during a campaign to make calls, request gifts, and reach goals.

Even though the basic principles are the same, there are four areas where your capital campaign will differ slightly from the annual campaign. An understanding of these key differences will help you evaluate the wisdom of conducting a capital campaign for your organization.

Purpose of Funds

Your annual campaign usually raises money to operate for a given fiscal year. It will cover salaries of employees, rent, utilities, and costs related to the services your organization provides. A capital campaign raises money to build a new building for your organization to utilize in providing its services to the community. It may include upgrading or adding to current facilities as well. Some capital campaigns are seeking to build an endowment fund that will be held by the organization utilizing only the interest earned to support its annual operation. It could include funds to purchase land for future expansion. In many cases, it may include any or all of the above.

Since your organization will only be conducting a capital campaign under normal conditions every 10 years or so, you need to do careful planning for the future. You may need an expansion to your existing facilities to expand your services for the next few years, but how long will it take you to outgrow even the additional space if you add it? Many organizations conduct long-range plans, seeking to analyze current operations and services and project future needs based on both historical experiences within the organization and anticipated changes within the community that should develop with community growth, changing economic conditions, and expanded demand for new services. Such a plan, if well done, will give your organization the information it will need to convince major donors of your need for the new building or the endowment. Therefore, if you believe you should consider a capital campaign, think big and look as far as possible into the future.

Size of the Goal

To plan and build for the future takes money. It takes much more than your organization currently raises to operate each year. Therefore your goal for a capital campaign will be much larger than the goal in the annual campaign. It would not be unusual for a capital campaign goal to be from 3 to 10 times larger than the amount you are currently raising for operations. There are no magic formulas, but be aware that there is a correlation between your organization's reputation and the community's willingness to support your capital campaign goal.

Actually setting the goal will be a function of assessing the organization's needs for capital expansion and the community's willingness to respond. Assessment of this willingness to respond will be discovered by conducting a feasibility study. Your needs will be fine-tuned by working with professionals such as architects, engineers, financial advisors, and contractors who can help you estimate how much it will cost to build the building or addition, or purchase the new equipment, or the earnings required from an endowment to ensure organizational stability. In other words, the campaign goal isn't just a multiple of your previous experience with fund raising, nor is it an uneducated guess about the price of new facilities. It's a careful blend of the needs of your organization and the potential to give within your community.

Remember a rule of thumb that has proven fairly accurate in capital campaigns all across the country by thousands of nonprofit organizations. A few major gifts, some of them "one-time-only gifts," will constitute the largest part of your campaign success. Some experts suggest the 80/20 rule. Eighty percent of your money will be contributed by 20 percent of your contributors. Others say 90/10. Some professional firms will want 8 to 10 gifts to total half or more of your goal. Many of your prospects may not now be annual supporters and may not become annual supporters. They will be wealthy individuals with a strong interest in your community and commitment to helping organizations such as yours serve that community. They may also include corporations and foundations that also make substantial gifts to enhance organizations as a part of their overall commitment to the institutions that make our society better.

Length of the Campaign

While the actual time of the solicitation of the prospects may not take much longer than your annual campaign, the planning and organizational efforts to conduct a capital campaign take much more time. The recruiting and training of volunteers will take much longer because a great many more volunteers will be needed to conduct the campaign. It is not unusual for an organization to start the initial planning for a capital campaign 2 or 3 years before the formal public announcement and kickoff of the campaign. Most professionals that help organizations raise capital funds not only spend a great deal of time in the planning and preparation phase of the campaign, but will want pledges and commitments in hand equaling a third or more of the goal before the public announcement.

Asking for a $1-million gift does not take much more time than asking for a $1000 gift, but getting the right prospect solicited by a top-notch community leader committed to the objectives of the campaign may take much longer than is the case in annual campaigns. Prospect research, cultivation, and volunteer training become much more important in capital campaigns. It could well take weeks or months to get the schedules of the prospective donor and the solicitor to match so a solicitation appointment can be set up. You can't get too many turndowns in a capital campaign and succeed. Matching the prospect and solicitor in the large gifts phase of the campaign is critical to your success. Don't rush it.

Because of the size of the goal, many capital campaigns have pledge periods from 3 to 5 years. The number of prospects personally solicited may well be five or six times more than in annual campaigns, and it would not be unusual for a very large campaign to last a year or more if you count the time it takes to conduct a feasibility study and the planning and preparations phase of the campaign.

Preparation and Leadership Needed

Recruiting and training a much larger group of volunteers than normal and the development of campaign materials means that much more time and effort is needed before actual kickoff of the campaign. Raising several million dollars takes top community leadership. Even in fairly large cities there are rarely more than 6 to 10 people that have both the capacity and commitment to lead major campaigns. Getting one of these key individuals may take months or in some cases years. As noted earlier, if you propose to build a building, architectural and engineering studies may play a key role in making your case. These also take time and money. In some cases, it may be necessary to strengthen the board of the organization with additional leadership and commitment before you can begin a campaign.

Attempting to start a capital campaign without a full understanding of the magnitude of the challenge will lead to failure. If your annual campaign is making it possible to raise the funds your board determines are the annual needs, it's much better to take the time necessary to build the reputation of your organization and its volunteer leadership so that your first attempt at a capital campaign is well planned and executed. Don't rush into a capital campaign to solve annual operating shortages. While a good capital campaign will tend to raise the giving levels of your regular supporters, a failure may stop your organization from trying again for capital funds for years.

What about Your Annual Campaign?

It is difficult to conduct a capital campaign and an annual campaign in the same year. You will use your annual donor base as a major component of your capital campaign. If your campaign excites large donors, it will excite your regular donors, and they will want to be a part of the campaign as well.

Most organizations recognize that it is complicated and confusing to ask annual contributors for two pledges to an organization at approximately the same time. The easiest way to solve this problem is to include, as a part of your capital campaign goal, the funds you would normally raise for annual operating expenses. For example, if you are currently raising $100,000 a year from your donors for annual operating expenses, and you would expect that figure to increase at about 10% per year, simply add annual operating funds to your campaign budget.

For example, if you will be taking pledges for the capital campaign over a 3-year cycle, total your operating needs as follows:

Year one	$110,000
Year two	$121,000
Year three	$133,100
Total for three years	$364,100

Rather than add the total figure to the campaign goal, recognize that you will need to return to the annual campaign process in year two and three and will be approaching regular prospects who did not contribute to the capital campaign. You will also be adding new prospects to your file. Therefore, discount the total taken from the campaign to help operating expenses. A good way is to discount year two by 40% and year three by 60%, as follows:

Year one	$110,000
Year two	$ 72,600
Year three	$ 53,240
Total	$235,840

A figure of $235,840 will become a part of your total campaign budget, noting that donors with outstanding pledges will not be solicited for annual support during years two and three. Once you reach your goal, transfer year one funds from your capital campaign fund to your annual operating fund. When you start your annual campaign in year two, transfer year two funds as a starting balance in the annual campaign fund.

Professional Help or Not?

Hopefully by now, you realize that conducting a large capital campaign is a big job. Few organizations have the professional staff on board to do all that is necessary to conduct such a campaign. That's not to say they do not know how or that they don't have the skills needed to conduct a campaign; but it does say that given their ongoing responsibilities for helping guide the securing of annual support, they normally do not have the time to give their undivided attention to a capital campaign.

Furthermore, both the staff and volunteers in most organizations have become so involved and committed to the success of the organization that it is difficult or perhaps impossible for them to maintain the objectivity necessary to conduct a good capital campaign. When conducting a feasibility study or developing a campaign plan, some tough questions must be asked of major sources of support in the community before a campaign can be successfully conducted. Major donors may have little understanding of what your organization does for the community despite your gallant effort at public relations. Your top volunteer leadership may be great from your perspective, but are they known and respected by the major financial supporters of your community?

Advantages of Professional Help

Professional firms, many national in scope, are readily available to your organization if you are considering a capital campaign. Even when you have an excellent staff component in your organization, it pays to have this outside and objective help when you conduct a campaign for large sums of money. In addition to conducting the all-important feasibility study, the professional firm can bring in the additional full-time staff help you need for the few months of the campaign, without causing you to add new staff positions that must be sustained over the years.

Cost of Professional Help

Good firms and individuals that follow the standards established by the American Association of Fund Raising Counsel, work for a fixed fee. It includes only charges for the actual time professionals on their staff work on your campaign and the related campaign expenses like secretarial help, printing costs, office rent, and travel and lodging expenses of employees assigned to the campaign. Although the fee may appear big, it should rarely exceed 10 to 15 percent of the campaign goal. No responsible professional in the field works on a commission that reflects a percent of goal. Anyone that suggests this approach should be avoided.

Most individuals and firms in the field will conduct a feasibility study for a fixed fee that again will recover only the costs of their time and expenses plus a reasonable profit. These fees will reflect mostly the time required to conduct the study. Conducting the study does not bind you to either the campaign or the firm that conducts the study. The study becomes the property of your organization, and can be used by you in any way you see fit.

Since very large campaigns will require more professional help to succeed, the fees for these campaigns will seem high by comparison, but they still are a small percentage of the campaign goal. Because some fixed costs charged by the firm are the same in campaigns of different sizes, the fee may actually drop as a percentage of the campaign goal when large sums are raised.

Selecting Professional Help

As when contracting for professional services in any business, it is a good practice to meet and interview several individuals or firms. Often a committee of the board can be productively involved. Discuss previous campaigns the firm has conducted and ask for references you can contact. Focus on campaigns they helped conduct that were done for organizations similar to yours. Ask each firm or individual to quote you a fee with a breakdown on how they arrived at the fee.

You can improve your process if you contact organizations in your community that have recently conducted capital campaigns and find out who they used and what their experience was. If your organization is affiliated with similar organizations around the state or country, contact some of them and ask similar questions. Many professional fund-raising consultants specialize in certain segments of fund-raising such as educational institutions, religious organizations, medical services, and human service organizations. Seek to interview representatives from some firms that specialize in your segment as a part of your pool.

Like other professionals, good fund raisers live or die on their reputations for honesty, effectiveness, and efficiency. They want to help you reach your objectives as efficiently as possible so they can assign their staff to new campaigns. Good firms and consultants will tell you the truth as they see it, even if it means a recommendation not to conduct a campaign at this time. Every assignment they take adds to their reputation in the industry. Even though their fee is fixed and they are paid whether you reach goal or not, they want to succeed as much as you do. They do not want to take a campaign that is destined to fail because of inadequate volunteer leadership, inadequate organizational identity in the community, or bad timing.

The Feasibility Study

Already in this chapter the feasibility study has been mentioned. It can play a key role in helping you determine when to start a campaign, how much you can reasonably expect to raise, and who you will need to lead the campaign. It will be a study of your organization, seeking to identify strengths and weaknesses that will affect a capital campaign effort. It will also study the external environment of your community to see how your community would react to a capital campaign for your organization.

What It Is

A good feasibility study will include a thorough analysis of your organization and its experience in offering services and raising money. The report will show trends over a period of years. Is your board effective? What size donor base do you currently have? Has the size of the donor base been increasing? How much volunteer leadership do you have to raise money? What are the skills of the employees, especially those related to fund raising? What records do you have? Are the records adequate to support a capital campaign? If you have conducted capital campaigns in the past, were they successful, when was the last one held, and what problems did you have? If appropriate, it will include information gathered from clients, alumni, or other recipients of your services. How do they feel about the work of your organization?

The external part of the study will seek to get a cross section of community response reflecting how well your organization is known and what value the service you provide has. It will be seeking to find out who potential leaders are for a capital campaign and their availability. Questions about timing will be asked. Is this a good time for an organization to raise capital funds? If a campaign were to be conducted, and you were approached for a gift, would you be inclined to make a contribution? What do you know about the leadership of the organization? Do you believe that the organization has a good cause to approach the community with?

Critical to developing a feasibility study are the skills of the interviewer. This is why it is almost always better to hire a professional. If you run into criticism about the services of your organization or of its leadership, it will be difficult to place the comments in proper perspective. Good studies may take 40 to 50 personal interviews, more if the goal is very large. Since community leaders must be personally interviewed, the whole process can be very time consuming. Depending on the person being interviewed and the time available, the interviewer must have the flexibility to meet changing schedules and know how to conduct the survey in the least intrusive style.

What to Expect

Once the interviews are completed and the figures gathered, a report will be written and presented to your organization. In almost all cases, it will recommend a campaign goal or goal range, identify top community leadership that can make the campaign successful, and will suggest a calendar and campaign budget to accomplish the objectives of the campaign. In some cases it may recommend that a campaign not be held until some corrective actions are taken. Increasing the number and effectiveness of the board, building a stronger community image, or building a larger donor base are often recommended.

If the study recommends a campaign, it often will be accompanied by a bid to conduct the campaign and a proposed budget. It should also include the number of days of professional help to be assigned to the campaign, and in most cases will name the individuals to be assigned to the campaign. It will also propose a starting date and a completion date. The bid should also include a provision for a final report from the campaign director and orderly transfer of all campaign records. Good campaigns will also include a follow-up system for collection of pledges and an audit of all activities.

When deciding on professional help and the appropriate fee, remember that some parts of the fee can be negotiated with the firm you choose. For example, the campaign will probably require office space that the organization does not have. Some firms will even insist, with good reason, that the office for the campaign not be a part of the regular office space of the organization because of confusion. The firm will be prepared to rent the space and the equipment needed for the few months it will be needed and will make the cost a part of their bid. If you can get comparable space and equipment donated for the campaign, they will normally be glad to use the space and equipment, and you will not be billed for these costs.

Once you and your board decide to conduct a campaign and hire a professional firm, be prepared to follow the advice and schedule adopted. More volunteer time by board members and staff will be required and everyone may feel pressed with new responsibilities. The campaign director is there to give leadership to your organization and its volunteers and staff, not to go ask for the money. He or she will be most insistent that deadlines are met and that commitments made by both staff and volunteers are kept. When deadlines are missed, corrective action will be taken quickly. In some cases, feelings will be hurt. It is not easy to raise substantial sums of money without a good deal of pressure. Establish an open and professional relationship with the people assigned to your campaign. When you don't understand something, ask questions. When you make a commitment, keep it. If you can't, let the campaign director know quickly.

Long-term Benefits of a Capital Campaign

Little is said in most of the literature about the long-term benefits of conducting a capital campaign. Everyone seems to assume that once the money is raised, it will be spent as stated and the facilities and/or services of the organization will be enhanced. Experience has shown that most good capital campaigns have additional benefits of value to the organization.

Increased Board Commitment

A good campaign almost always improves the quality and commitment of board leadership. They are excited about success, they have learned how to use their influence in getting help for the organization. Often you have identified community leadership, not previously active with your organization, that is now willing and perhaps anxious to join your board or otherwise become actively involved in activities of the organization.

Improved Staff Skills

Staff of the organization grow in their professional skills related to fund raising. They will do an even better job in guiding volunteers in the annual campaign in succeeding years.

Giving Levels Increase

Your current donors will have their giving sights raised. You will have asked almost all of them for increased personal contributions as a part of the campaign and they will, by giving more, become even stronger supporters of your cause. In most cases the increased giving levels will continue once the campaign pledge is paid. The net effect will be larger and more effective annual campaigns.

Donor Base Expanded

Your donor base will grow. You will be contacting many more prospects than you normally reach in an annual campaign. Some, by giving to the capital campaign, will become interested in your organization and can be included as a prospect in future annual campaigns once their pledges are paid. Even those people contacted as a part of the campaign and who did not give have learned about your organization. The awareness of who you are and what you do for the community has value to you. These prospects may also be good prospects for your annual campaign.

13

Raising Money with Projects and Memorial Gifts

There are many individuals, corporations, and foundations that find funding a project much more appealing than giving a gift to the annual campaign. These potential donors have different feelings about what they like to support, and often will provide you with a contribution for something that they can identify with that is tangible, defined in scope, or exciting to them personally. Some are motivated because it is a "one-time" gift. Therefore, identifying projects will improve your chances for a contribution with many donors that will not give to your annual fund.

Raising money with projects can be done as a special campaign or can be included in your annual campaign. You can easily set up a team of solicitors making calls on those prospects that will be more likely to give this way. With sufficient staff and volunteer support, there is no reason that project financing can't be conducted year round.

Steps in Selling a Project

As with any campaign, there are a series of steps that you must take to be successful. It is no different with projects. The principles of prospect identification and evaluation are the same as for an annual fund drive. Research is similar as well. The basic difference is the project. You are asking the prospective donor to give a gift that will be applied to a special project. Donors in the annual campaign are most often giving gifts to support the annual operating budget of your organization and no attempt is made to identify individual gifts.

Step 1—Identifying Projects

If you want to capitalize on getting support for your annual campaign from donors that under normal circumstances will not contribute, you *must* select projects that are included in your annual operating budget. That way, when you receive a gift for the project, you have covered a part of your operating budget and you have helped reach your goal for the annual campaign.

For example, if you must purchase a 15-passenger van for use in your program in the next fiscal year and you get a gift from a donor, either in cash or as an "in-kind" gift, you have secured a gift worth the cost of the van, say $15,000. You now have the van or the cash to buy it. You can count the gift toward the annual campaign goal or reduce the goal and your operating budget for the next fiscal year.

However, if you get a gift for a van or the actual van itself and you do not have such a purchase in your plans for the next fiscal year, you have not helped your annual campaign. It may be nice to have a new van, but it has not helped you secure your annual operating funds for the coming year. As you start developing your project financing program, keep this in mind.

List Possible Projects in Your Budget.   Look over your operating budget for next year for those items that make good projects—such things as equipment purchases, vehicles, recognition awards for volunteers, training material, expendable supplies related to client services, office supplies, special events or activities you will hold, and special services. Most of your projects will be tangible—canoes for camp, movie projectors, recognition plaques, typewriters, computers, training manuals, and paper—but not all need to be. How much does it cost for a day, week or month to serve a client? How much does it cost to train a camp staff member for your summer camp program? Items such as this can be good projects for some prospects.

Estimate the Annual Cost.   Take your list of projects and figure the actual cost for the project. Use reasonable estimates if calculating an exact cost is not practical. If you need a new typewriter, call a normal supplier and find out what a model that will fill your needs will cost. If the item will also have shipping costs, include those as well. A project to train a staff member would include the cost of the training conference, transportation, and lodging and meals as well. With large projects, it helps to list several categories of costs such as transportation, lodging, annual maintenance fees, or installation fees because the donor may like the project, but is unwilling to commit the whole asking price. A lesser gift can pay part of the cost and the rest of the project can be sold to another donor.

Develop a Range of Projects. Just as there are large donors and small donors in other campaigns, you will find this true in project selling as well. Make sure your list includes projects that have a wide range of prices. Look for projects that cost from $100 to $300, $300 to $500, and some mid-range projects at $1,000 to $2,500. Find some large projects also, $5,000 to $25,000.

Some projects are easy to develop and have "multiples." For example, if it costs you $100 per day to provide a client a day of service, that multiplies to $500 per week and $2,000 per month. Some prospects may buy a month of service while others may buy a day.

Step 2—Identify Prospects

Using the same principles of prospect identification and evaluation discussed in Chapter 4, start listing potential prospects. You can use the form shown in Chapter 1, Figure 1.1.

Identify first, those individuals, corporations, and foundations that will not support your annual campaign. They may be interested in a project. Next, list those current donors that have been giving at modest levels, but may upgrade their support for a project they can identify with. Also, list the names of individuals and companies that could provide a project as an "in-kind" gift. Finally, add the names of those vendors that do business with you. A company providing building cleaning services for you might give you a month of service free as a contribution.

Step 3—Research Your Prospects

As with the annual campaign, research your prospects before assigning them for solicitation. What is the connection to your organization? Do they have a history of supporting you in other areas? Do you have a volunteer who has a good relationship? What interests do they have? What size gift might the prospect give if called on by the right solicitor?

Step 4—Match Prospects with Projects

Compare your project list with your prospect list. Identify one or more prospects for each project. Also, list the names of prospective solicitors for each prospect. As with all campaigns, peer-to-peer solicitation is best. The larger the project, the greater the need for peer-to-peer personal solicitation.

Step 5—Write a Proposal

If there is a trick to project selling, it is the use of a written proposal. Such proposals work so well that when delivered by the appropriate solicitor, the project almost "sells itself."

The cover sheet for the proposal must say, "Especially prepared for (The individual, company or foundation name)" and must be typed. It must be short, well written, and professional in appearance. If you can read the proposal in 2 minutes or less, you have the right length—to state the need the prospect can identify with, the solution you offer, what the project will accomplish, and what you expect the results to be. Supporting the proposal should be a budget for the project in sufficient detail to give validity to the cost of the project, but not so detailed that it confuses the reader. For example, if transportation is involved in the project cost, simply list it that way and not as airfare, ground transportation and parking. With foundations and corporations, you will find it helpful to provide a list of your board members and a simplified copy of your most recent operating statement, audited if possible.

At the end of the proposal, but before the added documentation, add an "Acceptance Statement" to be signed by the prospect. This is the pledge card of project selling. By signing this statement the prospect has made a commitment to support the project with a gift of a specific amount by a specific date. Have an extra copy of the proposal with you so you can leave a copy with the prospect.

Special Note on Foundation Proposals. This chapter is dealing with project selling that will normally be directed to individuals and when fairly small in size, to some corporations and foundations. If you are making a major proposal to a foundation or corporation review Chapters 6 and 7. Foundations and corporations usually make grants to fund specific projects. If it is a major grant, it may require a larger, formal proposal with a lot of documentation. Understanding the foundationand/or corporation is important in this application. If either has a special presentation format, follow it.

Step 6—Deliver Your Proposal

Project selling is a good way to involve staff and volunteers as a team. While any good volunteer can make a presentation, it often helps to have staff accompany the volunteer on the call. Again, the larger the request the more this may be necessary. While it is important to keep the proposal short, questions may be raised that can best be answered by the staff member.

Call for an appointment. Once you have arrived and shared a few opening comments, hand the proposal to the prospect and *wait* for the person to read it. This may be the hardest part. If your proposal can be read in one or two minutes, simply be quiet. Answer questions as they are raised. Reinforce the proposal with personal experience with your organization if that seems necessary or helpful.

If you have done a good job of matching the prospect and the project, often the person will reach for a pen, sign the commitment, and give it back to you. If that happens, do what any good salesperson would do. Give a warm expression of personal thanks on behalf of your organization and leave. Follow-up with a thank you letter. If the prospect says no or asks for time to consider the proposal, ask if there are any questions you can answer and arrange a time to return. Even if you get a refusal, you may get some indication of what the prospect would respond to or perhaps a suggestion to submit the proposal at a later date.

Step 7—Continue Cultivation

Once the project is completed, send a report to the sponsor showing the results you achieved. Snap shots, if appropriate, make the connection even stronger. Remember, project sponsors like to identify with the project, and such a report helps the sponsor feel a connection to it.

If the project will take several months or years to develop, a quarterly progress report will keep your donor informed and happy. A final report is a must and may lead to new grants from the sponsor. Set up an office system to remind yourself to send these reports.

Special Aspects of Project Selling

In addition to the benefits already discussed, there are several additional benefits that make project selling an attractive addition to your annual giving program.

Multiyear Commitment

Normally gifts to your annual campaign are for the fiscal year. Projects often lend themselves to commitments of more than 1 year. A project may require several years to develop, implement, and evaluate. If so, a budget for 3, 4 or even 5 years would not be unusual. If the donor likes the project and understands the time necessary to complete the project, the commitment may be for the entire length of the project.

If you get a commitment of this type and the full cost is paid the first year, be sure to use only the funds for the first year. Place the remainder in a reserve fund for use during the appropriate year.

Gifts in Kind

Many companies find it easier to donate the actual equipment or supplies you need in lieu of cash. This can lead to gifts of equipment that you would have to buy anyway and give the donating company some tax advantages.

However, be careful when gifts in kind are offered. Does the gift really fill your needs? Is it the exact model you planned to buy or comparable to it? Is the equipment new or used? Is it state of the art and operational? Be aware that you can get someone else's problem.

It is best to establish a policy that your organization will accept donations of in-kind goods only if you can use the donations in your regular operations. If you find you can't, reserve the right to sell the gift and use the cash. Most donors, particularly those who want to donate used equipment, will not object to such a policy. Even then, be aware that picking up, storing, and selling the gift may cost more than you can sell it for. On more than one occasion I have had someone want to donate a "great" sailboat that turned out to be underwater owing to damage to the hull. Be careful!

Projects Are Often a Clear "Quid Pro Quo"

Most corporations are seeking some "quid pro quo" in their donations. Simply having their equipment used by people in your organization may enhance their corporate identity. That alone may be incentive enough to get the project funded. For example, restaurants often donate meals, and hotels, lodging, for the recognition it brings them.

Some projects, such as recognition awards for volunteers, have great public relations value to the company who sponsors the project. The award is presented with a card indicating the award was provided by a gift from the company and an additional expression of thanks to the volunteer by the company.

Project Donors Can Be Good Prospects for Other Campaigns

People who give you support for a special project become identified with you and your work. They become more knowledgeable of your success and therefore may become good prospects for annual gifts, capital campaigns, or larger projects in the future. With corporations, they may also lead to additional volunteer leadership for your organization.

Memorial Gifts Can Be a Steady Source of Income

Projects also have a special relationship to memorial gifts. On most any day in any fairly large city, the obituaries will carry listings asking that "in lieu of flowers, the family requests that gifts be sent to _____." Thousands of churches, synagogues, hospitals, and colleges have rooms, musical instruments, buildings, and furnishings given in memory of some loved one.

You can create a process in your organization that will invite people to make donations to your organization on a year-round basis if you set up a memorial gifts program.

Creating a Memorial Fund

Through board action, create a memorial fund. Establish policies for its operation, and develop the necessary material to support the program. Gifts can be used for more than bereavement. They can recognize achievement such as graduation from high school, college, or a professional school. Birthdays, anniversaries, promotions, and any special occasions where people want to express their good wishes are also appropriate. If a card or gift is appropriate for the occasion, a gift to the memorial fund may also interest the donor.

Establish Memorial Fund Policies

Establish operating policies for the memorial fund. How is the money to be used? Do you want it to become an endowment fund, using only the earnings each year? It usually helps the fund if you can tell people how the money is used. Your policies need to be flexible enough to accept sizable gifts with some stipulations by the donor.

Educate Members of Your Organization

Once you have established your memorial fund, start an ongoing educational program. Utilize a newsletter to announce creation of the fund. Tell people what type of occasions they can use to express their interest. Let them know how to give and what recognition the person, or the family will receive and what recognition the donor will receive. Ask members of the board to utilize the fund to help establish its existence.

Make it a practice to include such information in your newsletter on a regular basis when space is available. Your constituency needs to be told over and over again of the fund's existence.

Develop the Necessary Material

At the minimum, you will need two series of cards, both high quality and tastefully presented. First, you will need a series of cards to be sent to the person honored or the family of the deceased. This card tells the person or family that a gift to the fund has been received by your organization from the individual or organization listed on the card. The amount of the gift is *not* stated, except in unusual circumstances and then only with the permission of the donor.

A companion card is sent to the donor acknowledging the gift and stating that the person or family has been notified of the gift. The receipt for the gift can be enclosed in the same envelope. This card lets the donor know that the gift was received and the person or family notified of the gift. Figures 13.1 and 13.2 are examples of such cards.

A permanent record, suitable for review by the public, should also be established. Similar to a scrapbook, the book should have a dated entry listing the name of the person honored and the name of the donor. Such a book provides some tangible evidence of the existence of the memorial fund and should be on display in an appropriate place.

In addition to sending cards to the donor and the family or honoree, publish the names of donors to the fund on a regular basis in your newsletter or annual report. For example, you can list under a classification of "In Memoriam" the name of the deceased and below that, the names of all donors. This public recognition is important to both the family and the donor, and is another part of your ongoing educational program.

YOUR GIFT HONORING

HAS BEEN GRATEFULLY RECEIVED AS A PART OF THE BOY SCOUT
TRIBUTE FUND AND ACKNOWLEDGMENT HAS BEEN SENT TO

BE ASSURED THAT THIS GIFT SHALL BE REGARDED AS A SACRED
TRUST TO BE TRANSLATED INTO LIVING AND ENDURING MANHOOD

THE ATLANTA AREA COUNCIL
BOY SCOUTS OF AMERICA

DATE

SCOUT EXECUTIVE

Figure 13.1 Donor acknowledgement card (Courtesy of the Atlanta Area Council, Boy Scouts of America.)

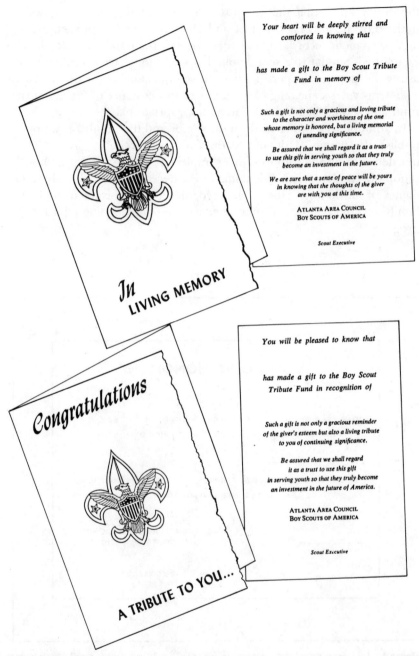

Figure 13.2 Congratulations and in living memory cards (Courtesy of the Atlanta Area Council, Boy Scouts of America.)

If you have a bookkeeping system or a fund-raising accounting system that will let you send donors annual statements of their gifts to the memorial fund, it will be yet another way of saying thanks and will generate future gifts to the fund.

Benefits of Establishing a Memorial Gifts Program

Although most gifts to your memorial fund will tend to be small, they add up, and can produce a steady flow of income if promoted with your constituency on a regular basis.

Many of your regular contributors will use the fund often if your recognition program fills their need to recognize a person or extend condolences to a special family. If you promote the program tastefully, it may lead to some large gifts as well.

It can also solve some bookkeeping problems for your organization. With the fund in existence, if a series of gifts come in that create some special memorial to an individual, usually deceased, you can deposit the funds in the memorial fund, acknowledge them, and not have to set up a special fund and the accounting support it will need unless the gift is large enough to be managed as a special fund. Colleges and universities find this "pooled" fund especially helpful with scholarships. Endowed scholarship funds must be quite large to provide enough earnings each year to provide a scholarship. By pooling small contributions, scholarships can be provided more efficiently. By having such a fund in place and a policy on minimum endowment for special scholarship funds, you can solve a donor's need immediately and perhaps lead to larger gifts at a later time.

Finally, a memorial fund also helps educate your constituency on the possibilities of endowments that come through planned or deferred giving programs. Chapter 11 has more on this subject.

14
Implications
of
Tax Reform

The Tax Reform Act of 1986

The Tax Reform Act of 1986 was enacted on October 22, 1986 and has been the most discussed tax law revision since the writing of the 1954 Internal Revenue Code. The full effects of the changes are still being analyzed and discussed. Most taxpayers will not feel the full implications of the act for several years as many of the changes will be phased in over a period of time.

During the fall of 1986 most nonprofit organizations were strongly advised by professional groups to inform their supporters of the implications of the coming tax changes and to point out the significant tax advantages for many donors to making contributions prior to December 31, 1986. At the same time, tax specialists and accountants were advising their clients to do careful tax planning to reduce the effects of the changes as much as possible prior to the end of the year.

As a result, most Americans who had previously supported charity were swamped with direct mail appeals to consider a contribution as 1986 drew to a close. The general assumption was that with the reduction in both the number of tax brackets and the marginal tax rates, the tax incentive to give in future years would be reduced. For many people, this assumption was true, but for others, particularly those taxpayers facing the Alternative Minimum Tax, it may not have been true.

While people were considering these additional appeals for contributions, they were also being exposed to large amounts of advertising suggesting that major purchases be completed before the end of the year because of the loss, as a deduction from adjusted gross income, of certain state and local sales taxes. In addition, investment counselors were advising the sale of greatly appreciated securities because of the 40 percent increase in the capital gain tax rate.

Basic Changes that Affect Charitable Giving

The act affects charitable giving by both individuals and corporations, with some changes to be phased in over several years, making it difficult to assess the full implications. Individuals and corporations are well-advised to seek professional help. Generally speaking, contributions of cash to charitable organizations by taxpayers who can itemize deductions continue to be fully deductible in determining taxable income. However, there are some subtle changes that can reduce the tax savings of a charitable gift.

Effects on Individuals

There are five areas where the new tax act affects individuals for 1987 and beyond.

Reduced Marginal Rates. Beginning in 1988, there will be a two-bracket rate schedule, 15 percent and 28 percent. During 1987 there are five brackets as a part of the phase-in program. The five-bracket rate schedule for 1987 will start at 11 percent and increase to a high of 38.5 percent. Table 14-1 shows the tax tables for individuals.

Many people will find that they are in a lower marginal tax bracket in 1987 and subsequent years. Assuming a lower marginal tax bracket, a charitable gift in 1987 and beyond will be more expensive for the giver because of decreased tax benefits. For example, if the taxpayer was in the 50 percent bracket in 1986, a gift of $1,000 would provide a tax savings of $500. In 1987, assuming the same taxpayer is in the 38.5 percent bracket, a gift of $1,000 would produce a tax savings of only $385, or a loss of $115 in tax savings over the previous year. If the taxpayer reaches the 1988 rate of 28 percent, the same gift in 1988 will provide tax savings of only $280, or a loss of $220 in tax savings over the 1986 rate.

Table 14.1. Income Tax Tables for 1987

Taxable income	Tax on col. 1	% on excess
Joint Return: Qualified Surviving Spouse		
$ 0	$ 0	11
3,000	330	15
28,000	4,080	28
45,000	8,840	35
90,000	24,590	38.5
Head of Household		
$ 0	$ 0	11
2,500	275	15
23,000	3,350	28
38,000	7,550	35
80,000	22,250	38.5
Single Returns		
$ 0	$ 0	11
1,800	198	15
16,800	2,448	28
27,000	5,304	35
54,000	14,754	38.5
Married Persons—Separate Returns		
$ 0	$ 0	11
1,500	165	15
14,000	2,040	28
22,500	4,420	35
45,000	12,295	38.5

SOURCE: Reproduced with permission from *1986 Tax Reform Act Highlights*, published and copyrighted by Commerce Clearing House, Inc., Chicago, Illinois.

Capital Gains Tax Rates. The highest capital gains tax rate has been increased from 20 percent in 1986 to 28 percent in 1987 and beyond. This means that a person selling a tangible asset will pay tax on a larger percentage of the increased value of the asset. In 1988 and beyond, this tax rate could go as high as 33 percent because of rate surcharges.

Even though a person still can give a charity a gift of an appreciated asset, pay no capital gains tax on the appreciated value, and claim the fair market value of the gift as a deductible gift, the reduction in marginal rates means the gift will cost the taxpayer more than in previous years. However, the increased capital gains rate will become more attractive as compared to cash gifts. Table 14.2 shows the effect of a gift of common stock under the old law as well as under the tax reform law. Should a contributor give stock with a fair market value of $1,000, the donor's cost is $468 as compared to $320 under the old law. This assumes, of course, that the donor recognizes the amount of capital gains tax that would have been paid had the asset been sold and then the gift made.

Additionally, the donor can deduct in the tax year an amount for contributions of appreciated property that does not exceed 30 percent of adjusted gross income. If the value of the appreciated gift exceeds 30 percent of the donor's adjusted gross income, excess deductions may be carried forward for up to five years.

Alternative Minimum Tax. The Alternative Minimum Tax has been a part of tax law since 1969. The new act raises the AMT rate only 1 percent for individuals to 21 percent. However, it is expected that many more people will be affected by this provision because "items of tax preference" (those items of income that must be added in determining the taxable base) have been increased and the marginal tax brackets have

Table 14.2. Gift of Common Stock

FAIR MARKET VALUE (FMV): $1,000
BASIS: $100
HOLDING PERIOD: Six months
Taxpayer not subject to alternative minimum tax

	Old Law	Tax Reform
Fair Market Value of gift	$1,000	$1,000
Basis	900	900
Tax Rate	50%	28%
Long-term capital gain exclusion	60%	0
Appreciation in value: FMV−basis	900	900
Reduction amount = 0	0	0
Deduction = FMV−reduction amount	1,000	1,000
Tax savings from deduction	500	280
Avoided tax on capital gain tax rate × appreciation	180	252
Total tax savings tax on capital gain avoided + savings from deduction	680	532
Cost of gift = FMV − tax savings	$320	$468

SOURCE: Susan Stern Stewart, "Major Tax Changes Affect Property Gifts," *Fund Raising Management,* November, 1986, p. 30.

been lowered. Further, a donor subject to the AMT that donates appreciated property will only be allowed the net tax benefit of deducting the cost basis of the gifted property in determining the tax base for calculating the AMT.

Loss of Charitable Deduction for Nonitemizers. The charitable deduction for nonitemizers was added to the tax code in 1981. This provision expired at the end of 1986, and there is no similar provision in the new act. Thus, nonitemizers will not be able to claim charitable deductions in figuring their taxable income. Furthermore, the new act has increased the standard deduction for individuals and it is likely fewer people will find it to their advantage to itemize their tax return.

Effects on Planned Giving. For the most part, rules covering trusts and similar devices in planned giving were not affected by the act. However, use of various deferred giving programs will become even more popular with donors, because of the increased tax rate on capital gifts. For example, a gift to a charitable remainder annuity trust, a charitable remainder unitrust, or a pooled income fund can still provide the donor tax-free transfer of his or her property.

The deferred gift annuity remains an appropriate vehicle in which income can be deferred and accumulated tax-free to start payment on a date that is near the expected retirement date of the donor.

As noted in Chapter 11, professional advice should be encouraged when any donor considers the possibility of using any of these vehicles as a way to make a gift to your organization and provide benefits to themselves or their beneficiaries.

The awareness of the general public about tax code changes will increase the number of people willing and anxious to analyze their financial affairs and will make planned gifts, using the techniques discussed in Chapter 11 even more attractive.

Effects on Corporations

As with individuals, corporations and the general business community were also affected by the Tax Reform Act of 1986. There are three areas which affect how a corporation or business organization makes a charitable gift.

Reduced Marginal Rates. Like individuals, the marginal rates for corporations have been reduced. For taxable years beginning on July 1,

1987, the maximum corporate tax rate will be reduced from 46 percent to 34 percent. As with individuals, this means now that it will cost the corporation more to make a charitable gift.

Gifts of Scientific Equipment from Inventory. Generally, when a corporation gives a gift from inventory to a charity, the deduction is equal to the property's cost, not its fair market value. Under some special limitations, gifts of certain scientific equipment can be given to colleges and universities and the deduction can be for the cost of the equipment and 50 percent of the fair market value. This rule was already in effect, but was extended to include scientific research organizations as eligible beneficiaries for such gifts.

University Basic Research. The original credit for corporate support of basic research expired in 1985. The new act extended the program but limited the credit to cash gifts. The value of equipment given to the charity is no longer deductible.

Motivations for Giving

The intense focus on the Tax Reform Act of 1986 overlooks the real motivations people have for giving their money away. Even though there are many predictions of greatly reduced income for nonprofit organizations in future years because of reduced tax benefits, there are many more reasons to be optimistic about the future.

Tax Benefits Are Not a Major Reason for Giving. Experience has shown over and over again that people who make charitable gifts on a regular basis, take advantage of the tax implications and tax consider-ations often affect the timing of gifts. However, only rarely is the tax issue a significant factor in the decision to make the gift.

A recent study conducted by Yankelovich, Skelly and White, Inc., and published by the Independent Sector in 1985 confirms that "tax deductibility" is not a major motivation for individuals who make contributions each year.

Two questions on this survey asked, "What would you say was the main reason you gave to (name of charity)? Anything else?" Answers that related to tax deductibility were so few in number that they were included in the other motives line shown in Table 14.3. As this table shows, people give for many reasons, but the most common reason for giving was that they considered a specific cause worthy or had some personal interest in it. This was followed closely by the desire to help the poor, needy, and less fortunate.

Table 14.3 Motives for Giving

	Total (percent)
A worthy cause/interest in the function of the charity/charity helping my favorite groups	13
Helps poor, needy, less fortunate	12
Deductible from salary	10
Close involvement, loyalty with the organization/ personal experience	10
Provides money for many causes	7
Feel obligated/responsible	7
Does good, reputable work/has quality programs	6
Spiritual reasons	6
Death or illness of a relative or personal friend	5
Has good organization, administration, control	5
Involved in local community	4
Being asked/responded to appeal	4
Other motives	11
Total	100

SOURCE: Virginia Ann Hodgkinson and Murray S. Weitzman, *The Charitable Behavior of Americans*, Independent Sector, Washington DC, 1985.

A Profile of Large Givers.   The Yankelovich study discovered a number of factors about people who give money away each year. A large giver was defined as someone who gave away $500 or more during the year.

Their study of this group showed that 89 percent give regularly, and they support several different charities. Their biggest gifts are to their church, with the second largest support going to education. They respond best when they are asked personally by someone they know. Over 75 percent said they were likely to give when approached this way. They give more when they can pledge rather than give a cash gift. They particularly like to be able to make gifts through payroll deductions.

Large givers are likely to be married or widowed, have higher levels of education, and are between 50 and 64 years of age.[1]

Notes

1. Virginia Ann Hodgkinson and Murray S. Weitzman, *The Charitable Behavior of Americans: Findings from a National Survey*, Independent Sector, Washington, D.C., 1985.

Index

About the Author

Ted D. Bayley is vice president for development and alumni affairs at Georgia State University, and he acts as a consultant, speaker, and seminar panelist on fund raising. For 18 years he was a full-time professional employee of the Boy Scouts of America, involved in a variety of fund-raising activities—from successful annual campaigns to special events. He has also worked as a volunteer fund raiser for nonprofit organizations such as the United Way and the National Alumni Association. ·